Surviving and Thriving With Parkinson's

A practical guide to living well from a 20-year Parkinson's survivor.

Briony Cooke

"Parkinson's Disease was a route I didn't choose, but a journey I had to make; there was no backing out. But I began to realise that there was a choice about how I would travel."

Copyright © 2018 Briony Cooke

ISBN: 978-0-244-36140-2

All rights reserved, including the right to reproduce this book, or portions thereof in any form. No part of this text may be reproduced, transmitted, downloaded, decompiled, reverse engineered, or stored, in any form or introduced into any information storage and retrieval system, in any form or by any means, whether electronic or mechanical without the express written permission of the author.

Acknowledgements

Orion, the pharmaceutical company who gave me permission reproduce the blogs which originally appeared on its website wearingoff.com between 2012 and 2014.

PEPS (Positively Enthusiastic Parkies) is a young onset Parkinson's support group in Reading, UK. The group, which was created in 2007 is affiliated to the Reading Branch of Parkinson's UK. Members whose blogs are featured here include:
Nigel Crabb – Customer Services Manager
Margaret Deacon - Departmental Administrator, Finance and Resources, University of Reading. (Retired).
John Inglis – Vodafone (Retired)
A former airline pilot (anonymous)
Howard Jarvis - Clerk of Works, University of Reading (Retired).
Kathie Smallwood - Expert Patient and Tutor, Oxford University.

Other contributors:
Dilys Parker - Community Nurse and Educator
Karen Green - GP (Retired)
Editor: Henry Cooke (Retired)
Editor: Katie Cooke
Illustrator: Jane Upton
Photographer: Doug Upton.
Production Manager: David Lewis, Publisher (Retired)
IT advisors: Robert Hine and Chris Cooke.
Project advisor: Alix Latchford. – Physiotherapist (Retired)
Web Designer: Tom Upton

My grateful thanks to the Neurologists, Neurosurgeons and Advanced Nurse Practitioners at The John Radcliffe Hospital, Oxford. Their surgical skills and expertise have enabled me to manage PD and to write this book.

About the Author

I was 47 when I was diagnosed with PD in 2000 although my symptoms became apparent about five years previously. At the time, I was subject leader for geography and environmental science in a tertiary college.

Teaching with PD, both in and out of the classroom, was stressful. At this time, I was in a new role of Senior Tutor to 250 students and was responsible for their university applications.

Although I had always loved teaching, the combination of classroom delivery, tiring fieldwork and endless marking at home forced me to take early retirement in 2006.

Out of college, I was also Deputy Chief Examiner for geography with the International Baccalaureate and travelled widely to promote the course to geography teachers in Europe, Africa and the Middle East. This work was varied and rewarding and involved curriculum review, exam paper setting and marking, but by 2008 it became too demanding and I retired.

Retirement has been rewarding and fulfilling and gave me unexpected opportunities: I have been the co-author of five geography textbooks.

I have been married to Henry, a journalist, for 41 years. We have three grown-up children, two grand-children, two cats and four tortoises.

I have survived Parkinson's unrelenting punishment, but I am not beaten yet. Writing this book has been my ambition.

Contents

Chapter 1 Introduction
1.1 The benefits of reading this book
1.2 Aims in writing this book
1.3 The organisation of this book
1.4 Terms used in this book

Chapter 2 The Diagnosis
2.1 Diagnostic tests for PD
2.2 Early symptoms
2.3 The path to diagnosis
Blog: Pretence
2.4 Blog: Diagnosis Day – Briony Cooke
2.5 Blog: Diagnosis Day – Margaret Deacon
2.6 More experiences
2.7 Emotional changes
2.8 Frequently asked questions
2.9 Blog: Reflections on the early days

Chapter 3 Telling others
3.1 Reactions and responses
3.2 Blog: I'm OK, thanks.
3.3 Accommodating PD

Chapter 4 The facts and the myths; what PD is and is not.
4.1 What is PD?
4.2 What are the risk factors?
4.3 Prevalence
4.4 Common myths
4.5 Raising awareness
Blog: Shaking out the misconceptions.

Chapter 5 Taking control
5.1 Medication - managing Levodopa

5.2 The complications of Levodopa
5.3 Blog: The roller-coaster ride
5.4 Managing protein with Levodopa
5.5 Other medication
5.6 The treatment of non-motor symptoms
5.7 Diet and digestion
5.8 The importance of exercise
5.9 Blog: Support groups

Chapter 6 Other options
6.1 Clinical trials
6.2 Blog: Dilys Parker's experience of clinical trials
6.3 Introduction to Deep Brain Stimulation (DBS).
6.4 Blog: Holes in the head
6.5 Effects of DBS 9 months later
6.6 Post-operative assessment 2014-2016
6.7 Second chance

Chapter 7 Facing the future
7.1 Objective measurements of PD.
7.2 My timeline
7.3 Timeline detail
7.4 Blog: The "Honeymoon" years
7.5 Blog: Then and now

Chapter 8 Minding the brain
8.1 Anxiety
8.2 Blog: Panic
8.3 Depression
8.4 Communication breakdown
8.5 Invisibility
8.6 Dementia

Chapter 9 Issues and practicalities
9.1 Domestic deskilling
9.2 Blog: Yuletide challenge
9.3 Work and early retirement
9.4 PWP experiences
Nigel Crabb
Margaret Deacon
Howard Jarvis
A former airline pilot (anonymous)
9.5 Journeys with PD
Blog: Beating the queues by John Inglis
Blog: Karen Green - The benefits of cruises for PWP
Blog: On the buses
9.6 Sleep problems with PD – insomnia and somnolence
Blog: Nodding off
9.7 Blog: Me and RBD

Chapter 10 Mustn't grumble
10.1 Distractions
10.2 Blog: Life in the slow lane
10.3 Emotions, endorphins and music
10.4 Blog: Music, music, music
10.5 PD and personality
10.6 Attitudes
10.7 Blog: The emotional value of chocolate
10.8 Blog: Looking on the bright side
10.9 Tribute to Tom Isaacs

Chapter 11 Parkinson's: a laughing matter
11.1 Parky games
11.2 Achievements

Final conclusions
Glossary
Appendix
Types of help
Benefits for PWP in the UK
International contacts

Chapter 1
Introduction

This chapter explains my objectives in writing this book.

1.1 The benefits of reading this book

Parkinson's can badly wreck your plans. You have no idea of how it will behave and how long it will be before it renders you disabled.
But neither is it a death sentence. Living well with Parkinson's is a huge challenge, but this book will describe how this can be achieved.
The book is born of 20 years of living with PD and experiencing the difficulties encountered by its progression, both mine and those of friends with the disease.
There are plenty of medical books written by PD experts with an abundance of factual information. But few of these authors live with the disease day in, day out.
Inevitably, such books are also heavy on pharmaceutical and medical terms. They expect readers to understand not only the language, but also the concepts.
This book does not cover the scientific complexities of the disease, and its use of medical terms and concepts is limited to those which you are likely to meet at the neurology clinic. At the diagnosis stage and beyond, my need was for palatable information written by the patient. I wanted to know how it felt to live with PD. I wanted this first-hand.
My book does not consider current research and the drive towards a cure. To cover this topic adequately would require a further book and a level of expertise that I do not have. A brief discussion of this topic would be inadequate and it might falsely raise the hopes of newly diagnosed PWP.

1.2 Aims:
To recognise the variety of symptoms and treatments for PD

PD is a very complex disease with a range of symptoms affecting people in different ways. For example, tremor affects only 30% of patients and yet the general public regards it as dominant. Very few people know that there are secondary symptoms such as poor balance and gastric reflux. Unfortunately, the full physical and psychological impact of PD is seldom realised or acknowledged. There's no one-size-fits-all when it comes to Parkinson's treatment. But the information in this book is a reliable basis for understanding this disease. The blogs and diary entries give some insight into my daily life and that of the other contributors. They show that symptoms and experiences can vary between individuals, and they are not necessarily common to all.

There is particular focus on young-onset patients diagnosed under 50. Many must cope with the demands of a family, full-time job as well as well as a chronic illness.

The book is designed to interest others who are affected by the disease, such as caregivers and family members.

To address misconceptions about PD

To look on the internet for PD, you'd be forgiven for thinking it only affects old men, that its symptoms involve shuffling and shaking, and that it is a rather trivial condition. In **Chapter 4**, I will challenge these impressions not only because of their inaccuracy, but also because the image of PD as a debilitating and devastating disease is underplayed. If its status and image were changed, PD would attract more attention and funding should follow.

To review the symptoms and how to manage them

The book covers the treatment of symptoms using conventional drugs, surgery, exercise and alternative therapies.

To evaluate other approaches involving patient choice
My experience of surgical treatments such as Deep Brain Stimulation is also covered here. I will look back at the decision-making that led up to surgery, and analyse the outcomes.
Dilys Parker (PWP) also reviews clinical trials in this chapter. She explains the choices that she had to make.

To examine the links between mind and body
With more advanced disease, PD suffers can become seriously socially isolated and invisible, and pre-existing mental health issues can be compounded by Parkinson's.
I will analyse psychological symptoms such as anxiety and depression, including how to manage them.

To define useful terms in a Glossary
The Glossary defines key terms regularly used by clinicians, but often misunderstood by patients and their caregivers.

To recognise that, although PD is no laughing matter, we need to look on the bright side
Humour is a tonic and distracting ourselves with hobbies and diversions is part of the recipe for survival.

Caveat
In writing this book, I've been conscious of how lucky I've been. Parkinson's is a cruel disease and like all diseases it is indiscriminate in whom it affects and when. But I'm lucky to have a strong, supportive family and great friends, who'll listen to me and help me out. I know not everyone is so lucky. For some PWP, just leaving the house is impossible. Getting to a hospital is impossible. Getting recognised and getting the help they need is impossible and it's for those people I'm writing this book.

1.3 The organisation of this book.

The book contains factual information in the main text and experiences and opinions in the blogs. The majority of these blogs are written by the author (shown in italics), but others have also contributed and their names are given in the blog title. The blogs provide the reader with the patient's perspective on aspects of PD presented in the text. Their order is topic-based rather than chronological.

Each chapter is introduced at the start and its contents outlined. At the end, most have a Review focusing on key points made and throughout the book there are questions to check your understanding.

1.4 Terms used in this book
PD: Parkinson's Disease
PWP: Person/People With Parkinson's

Chapter 2
The diagnosis

Introduction:
A diagnosis of Parkinson's is a tremendous shock. In this chapter, I'll discuss how Parkinson's is diagnosed, and will take you through what led up to my diagnosis back in the summer of 2000, as well as how I dealt with the shock and immediate aftermath of that day. In this chapter, you will find several Blogs written by PWP and your will notice that their experience varies.

2.1 Diagnostic tests for PD
There is no one way to diagnose PD. However, there are various symptoms and diagnostic tests used in combination. One of the most important things to remember about diagnosing PD is that there must be two of the four main symptoms present over a period of time for a neurologist to consider a PD diagnosis.

The four cardinal (key) symptoms are:
Shaking or tremor
Slowness of movement, called (bradykinesia)
Stiffness or rigidity of the arms, legs or trunk
Trouble with balance (postural instability) and possible falls.

The examination by a neurologist remains the first and most important diagnostic tool for patients suspected of having PD. Very often an MRI scan will have been arranged to eliminate other possible causes for your neurological symptoms, such as a brain tumour. The neurologist will make the diagnosis based on:

A detailed medical history and physical examination and a detailed history of your current and past medications, to make sure you are not taking medications that can cause symptoms similar to PD.

A detailed neurological examination during which a neurologist will ask you to perform tasks to assess the agility of arms and legs. The neurologist will also assess your muscle tone, gait and balance.

You may notice that a neurologist records your physical status in a table, called United Parkinson's Disease Rating Scale (UPDRS). (See Glossary).

The response to medications (that imitate or stimulate the production of dopamine) causing a significant improvement in symptoms is how the diagnosis of PD is made clinically.

2.2 Early symptoms
Tremor
This is a slight shaking in your finger, hand or lip. The tremor is most noticeable in your hand when it is at rest. When you take exercise it may stop. Shaking may also be caused by medication that you take, and is not limited to PD.

Small handwriting (micrographia)
A change in handwriting so that it becomes smaller and less legible may be an early symptom of PD.
Of course, there may be other causes such as stiffness in the hand or poor eyesight.

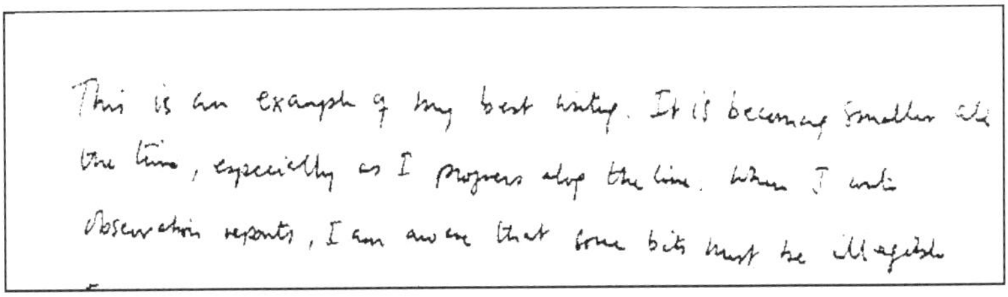

> *This is an example of my best writing. It is becoming smaller all the time, especially as I progress along the line. When I write observation reports, I am aware that some bits must be illegible*

Fig 1 The author's illegible handwriting in 2001 before medication improved dexterity and reduced stiffness.

Loss of smell (anosmia)
A change of smell or a reduction in ability to smell is a typical early sign of PD. You need not assume immediately that you have PD especially if there might be another cause such as cold or flu which makes your nose stuffy.

Stiffness and slowness in moving around and walking (bradykinesia)
This is particularly noticeable at night and first thing in morning. The shoulder is often the area that is affected and that means you may not swing the arm involved. It may occur when starting to move or changing direction. Your mind wants to move, but your limbs do nothing and thus you may topple over.

Constipation
PD affects every part of your body and even at this early stage you may notice constipation is a problem. The movement within your intestinal tract (gut motility) usually slows down in PD. There are many other causes including medication to treat PD.

Soft and low voice
People may tell you that you are difficult to hear but you don't see the problem. At the same time, you may claim that your

spouse or partner has a hearing problem that there is nothing wrong with your voice. This creates a huge amount of stress and argument. You should talk to your doctor about your voice and how he/she perceives it and your partner should seek a hearing test. This should reveal the answer. You may find that no-one is to blame and you both have slight deficiencies.

Masked face
PD affects the muscles in your face, resulting very often in a deadpan look and lack of blinking. This may create an off-putting expression, causing people to think that you are either sad or angry. (See chapter 8)

Stooped posture
This is a result of the contraction of muscles in your back and legs so that you develop a stoop. This may also be the result of postural imbalance.

Non-motor symptoms – these are common symptoms which can occur at any stage of the disease. They do not involve movement.

2.3 The path to diagnosis
Blog: Pretence by Briony Cooke
The onset of the disease is very slow and somewhat insidious. It creeps up on you, and gradually you begin to notice the persistence of a particular symptom. For me these were stiffness and tremor on my left side.
About five years prior to diagnosis I went to a chiropractor because of the stiff back and neck. I also tried a physiotherapist who specialised in sports injuries and another who made me a mouth guard supposedly to realign my jaw, but this came to nothing but a large bill. I had my back scrunched and twisted but it did not improve. The symptoms persisted and I could contain

my curiosity no longer. I would be brave and consult the oracle; an old tatty paperback of medical symptoms last referred to when expecting babies. I found "Parkinson's disease" and for an uncomfortable moment I noticed the similarity between my symptoms and theirs, but of course I was far too young to get it. So, I shut the book and dismissed the idea, at least for a while.

Between January and June 2000, I was still bothered by pain in my back and my stiff left arm. I arranged some physiotherapy near the college so didn't interrupt my day too much and I could pop over at lunchtime. The physio manipulated me and looked pensive. She advised me to see my GP and to see a consultant neurologist at the local hospital. I did so and the neurologist talked about chemical imbalances in my brain. He never mentioned the word Parkinson's, but he asked me to come back for an MRI brain scan. I was not worried.

2.4 Diagnosis Day

The two blogs and patient survey that follow recount the events of Diagnosis Day. You will see that there is a wide range of experiences and the impacts upon the person with Parkinson's (PWP).

Blog: Diagnosis day – August 8, 2000 by Briony Cooke
I had received a letter from the hospital telling me that my brain scan had been normal, and that I should come for a second appointment with the consultant neurologist. This was just a formality and nothing to worry about, I said to myself. So, I went alone to my consultation.
After a while reading stale copies of Woman's Own, *I was called into the consulting room where I found a second doctor waiting there. She was not a student and I wondered why the consultant*

wanted a second opinion. We went outside the office he asked me to walk down the corridor. The two doctors nodded and the other disappeared.
We returned to his room and he talked about my neurotransmitters and basal ganglia. Then he finally mentioned PD. But the two words which stuck in my brain were "progressive and incurable". For a moment, I was stunned.

The questions I asked him - to which he could not give definite answers - were:
"Will I go bonkers?" He hoped not.
"Will I have to stop driving?" Not yet.
"How long will I be able to work?" It was difficult to say.
The consultation then became more reassuring. The progression would be slow and for some years I could continue my life without any major changes. Just as I was beginning to feel better about it he said while shaking me by the hand on parting -"I'm sorry". That did it; I was in deep trouble.

I had come alone to the hospital and this department had no-one who might rescue me after such a devastating diagnosis. There was no-one else to turn to; no one to pick up the emotional pieces as I walked down the ice blue hospital corridor with my diagnosis and new identity at 11a.m. on August 8, 2000. I was alone and had to confront the world with my bad news. I rang my husband at work and he was shocked and disbelieving that I had been diagnosed with a geriatric disease at 47. He came straight home and we were lost for words.

That afternoon I scoured the Internet to find what lay ahead for me. I have always been one to find out the truth and to confront the horrors.
I found a glossary of PD symptoms and worked my way through:
Anxiety – I already had plenty of that.

Basal ganglia – a bit of my brain with an explanation went right over my head.
Cog-wheeling – was not a sport but a "gross motor" symptom, whatever that meant. It all sounded fairly "gross" to me.
Reflecting on my afternoon's research I decided how I would deal with this condition. I would keep a stiff upper lip, keep smiling and carry on, but whatever happened I was not going to drool. You wouldn't find me dribbling in a wheelchair. This was going to be a "mind-over-matter" job.

It was the summer holidays and that day our two teenage sons returned home tired and hungry from their holiday jobs. When I blurted out my news they were quite shocked. I played down the nasty bits and emphasised that it would be business as usual and normal domestic services would resume shortly i.e. the dinner. At about 11 p.m. our daughter returned having celebrated her 22nd birthday that day. I watched her face fall as I dropped the news on her but despite the shock, she was strong and supportive. How lucky I was to have a family who cared.

Telling the rest of the family was difficult. My mother lived 120 miles away and my brother with his family in Ohio, USA. I had discussed neither my symptoms nor my hospital appointments, so the news came as quite a shock to both.
My sister, however, lived nearby and would cope. She was able to turn any crisis into a comedy. As an amputee since the age of 28, she had laughed her way through life and disability. She had survived and risen above this indignity and I wanted to be like her.

PD was a route I didn't choose, but a journey I had to make; there was no backing out. But I began to realise that there was a choice about how I would travel. I could wallow in self-pity and enter a downward spiral of depression or I could pick up the pieces and attempt to continue life as usual. I chose the latter. I decided that PD might cramp my style, but it was not going to crush my spirit.

Fig. 2 Briony Cooke, 2000; the year of diagnosis.
Source: Doug Upton

Blog: Diagnosis Day - January 2007, by Margaret Deacon
Before my PD diagnosis, I had experienced some abnormal sensations which were giving me cause for concern:
I had noticed that my footing was becoming a problem whilst walking upstairs. The grip on my left foot had become weaker to the extent that I would lose a slip-on shoe.
If I stretched out my left arm I would experience a slight tremor. I began to lose some grip in my left hand which was affecting my handwriting.

I had recollections of my grandmother sitting in her chair when we went to visit her when I was about eight years old. She would attempt to hold her cup which would rattle in the saucer. Her hand would be shaking and we were told that she was unwell and had to take medication for a disease called Parkinson's.

Although the thought had crossed my mind, I certainly didn't want to believe that I was going to follow in my grandmother's footsteps. I tried to convince myself that my symptoms would not be attributable to PD. I had read that the disease wasn't hereditary.

On a routine visit to my GP, I plucked up the courage to tell him about my symptoms and my grandmother's illness. After a short conversation and completing a few physical exercises he advised me that he would refer me to a neurologist. I didn't know what to think. Was I being referred purely as a precaution or did my GP have the same doubts as me? I would have to wait and see.

My appointment day arrived and I sat in the waiting area of the Neurology Outpatients department with my mum who came to keep me company but we had agreed that I would go and see the consultant on my own. After what seemed to be an eternity, my name was called. I thought, I must walk upright with confidence to demonstrate that my symptoms were minor.

The neurologist held out his hand to introduce himself. Then, I agreed to a student being present during my appointment.

First, I was asked to explain my symptoms and the reasons why I had suspected that they might be linked to PD. The next stage was to undergo some cognitive tests and walk up and down the room. Following the tests, I was asked to have a seat. What came next was no surprise to me but it didn't lessen the blow. The consultant told me that my suspicions had been correct and my symptoms were relevant to PD.

My first question was to ask about the prognosis. I was 55 years of age and I had a lot of living to do! I had two wonderful grandchildren who I wanted to see grow up and to be a big part of their lives. I also had very good job. Would I have to give it up and how would we manage? My husband and I had planned to do some travelling when we retired and visit relatives in Canada. My head felt as though it was being crushed with the whirlwind of emotions I was experiencing.

The consultant advised me to fulfil our retirement plans as early as possible as the next ten years would be the best. I was given advice on starting on medication and the regime for appointments at the Neurology clinic. I was given the name of the PD Nurse and details of a local support group for young people with early onset of PD who meet upon a monthly basis.

At the end of the appointment the consultant wished me all the best and I walked back to meet my mother in a daze. We went for a cup of tea and I told her the news. Now I had to face the rest of the family and be prepared for the questions and answers. Everyone was supportive. I resigned myself to the fact that if PD is to be a part of my life so be it, but it would not rule my life. I have a motto which keeps me going "Live for today, look forward to tomorrow and forget about yesterday."

2.6 More experiences of diagnosis by the PEPS* support group members.

A survey was carried out in June 2017 at a meeting of the local young onset group involving 15 members. The intention was to gather information about the way in which this news (a diagnosis of PD) was delivered, by whom, and its consequences.
Those who were interviewed had been diagnosed between 2 and 20 years ago. Sometimes the GP was involved in the initial

diagnosis, but this was followed by a hospital referral and confirmation by the consultant neurologist.
The majority of those interviewed were unhappy about the whole diagnostic process on a number of accounts:

It was too short, with some consultations lasting just 10 minutes. The average was 25 minutes.

Explanations were brief, but the terminology was complex.

There was no additional support immediately after diagnosis such as the PD Nurse.

Several of those interviewed asked for a second consultation to clarify what had been said.

The diagnostic procedure could have been improved in several ways:

It may not be possible to ensure that the patient is accompanied by a friend or relative, but the provision of support such as a PD Nurse to "pick up the pieces" after the consultation, is essential and was missing in most cases.

A booklet might give the patient an outline of the condition without overwhelming them with unfamiliar medical terms.

*PEPS (Positively Enthusiastic Parkies) is the young onset support group for Parkinson's UK in Reading, Berks.

2.7 The emotional changes in attitude to diagnosis over time.

Shock
PD is an incurable, progressive and chronic disease
which is a terrifying prospect for some PWP
especially those who are under 50.

Disbelief
Why me?
Initially, you may feel bitter and resentful
and you may begin to envy others who are not so afflicted.

Confusion
You receive advice from many directions
and you become overloaded and confused
with different suggestions and advice.

Anxiety
You are not happy with your new identity as a sick person
and you worry that your symptoms may become apparent in
public and let you down.

Resistance
You have learnt the basics of managing this disease
and now you want to fight back.
You start campaigning and improving public awareness of this
disease.

Resignation
This is a reluctant form of acceptance.
You realise that PD is not going to go away but it will become a
way of life

2.8 FAQs by the newly diagnosed Person with PD
Who am I?
"You have Parkinson's". The three words that cut through your consciousness are still embedded in your brain. You won't forget that day. For many the diagnosis is unexpected and deeply shocking and there is a feeling of bewilderment and overwhelming uncertainty. You are no longer who you were; your identity is threatened along with your confidence and self-esteem. Instead of being the nurse, the sales assistant, the web designer or the trucker, you are "that person with PD". This is how it might feel if you are newly diagnosed, but in time you will recover the old "you" as PD becomes a way of life.

Why me?
Being diagnosed at any age with a progressive and incurable disease may lead to feelings of resentment and even anger, especially if you are under 50 and have a family and financial responsibilities. You may wonder what you have done to deserve such a life-sentence. If this is how you are feeling, it's time to take stock and focus on the positive: what you still have rather than what you have lost. It may also be a good idea to look around you and see the burdens that others carry. You may well change your mind and ask yourself the question "Why *not* me?"

Whom should I tell?
Telling people your bad news is a duty, but you can take it in easy stages. First there's your family. The diagnosis may be a surprise to them and your partner, but they need sympathy because they too are having to come to terms with the lifestyle changes and the prospect of caring for you one day. Spare your children the bad news and reinforce the notion of "business as usual". Responses are usually reassuring, but be prepared for the negative response. Remember that the person responding was not prepared for the

shock. There never seems to be an ideal place or time to give bad news, but the sooner people know, the more support you will get. Telling your employer in the first instance is not essential. But as time goes on and your symptoms become obvious, it may be in your interest to do so.

How long does it take before life becomes difficult?
With PD, the rate of progression is difficult to determine and varies between individuals. The symptoms may remain mild and unchanged for decades, but this is unusual and only 5-10% of cases experience little disability during the first 10 years. Alternatively, progression may be rapid in 5-10% of the population and the patient will become wheelchair-bound and totally dependent on others for their care and well-being.

What does my future hold?
Researching PD and finding out all you can about the condition will help you to manage it successfully. All sorts of questions may pass through your mind: How is PD going to affect my life expectancy? Will I lose my marbles? It may be frustrating that you cannot find answers to these questions because PD is a designer disease which affects all of us in different ways. By all means trawl the Internet, but be prepared for some home truths and baffling terms in medical literature.

Who can help me?
Despite all the uncertainties of coming to terms with such a diagnosis, there is hope. Health professionals such as PD nurses and local support groups run by volunteers can provide problem solutions and information. Many find contact with other people with PD very helpful because they can empathise with the trauma of diagnosis and point new patients in the direction of the health professionals. A local support group can offer you plenty of

information, advice, friendship, therapies and lots of social contact. (See Appendix)

How do I stop thinking about it?
Distraction is a good way of managing PD and preventing it from taking over your life. Once you have come to terms with your diagnosis, find ways of keeping your mind off the topic and develop new interests. Some more active pastimes can be continued for many years such as badminton and golf. PWP can also benefit from local creative groups. You may be reluctant to join a class because of fear about people noticing your tremor or stiffness. Most likely, they will not notice, but if they do, it's best to tell all and you will probably find that they are very understanding and you will feel relieved.

What now?
Your self-esteem can be badly damaged by the diagnosis. It can demoralise and demotivate, but this will not last if you take control and actively manage your condition. There will of course be bad days when you slip into self-pity and fear of the future overwhelms you, but this will not last and you must remind yourself that tomorrow will be better.
One thing is certain, things will only get better as you come to terms with having PD and realise that the diagnosis is not the end of the world, but a change of direction. The skills that you may have lost can be replaced by new ones. The uncertainties you experienced before diagnosis are over: you have an identified condition which can be treated, and you can look forward to some good times ahead.

Question
Look through the FAQs above and explain why loss of identity is a common feeling among the newly diagnosed.

2.9 Blog: *Reflections on the early days* by Briony Cooke
The other day, while sorting out books, I came across a number of diaries I had kept since 1978. Thirteen volumes about life's great events: pregnancies, blow-by-blow accounts of baby deliveries, infant development month-by-month and annual family holidays. They were full of amusing anecdotes, moments of parental pride and embarrassment. The first diaries were written during my seven years at home with three young children. These were my "playschool years" when I enjoyed all diversions from housework, but might have forgotten how to string a sentence together had I not kept writing. Later on, I recorded our holidays: carefree days of adventure and exploration staying at pig farms, remote crofts or surrounded by sheep and sunshine (if we were lucky).

Among these diaries of family fun was a more recent and more serious one started in August 2000: "Parky's Progress – a diary of defiance". Here were my first 11 years of living with PD diligently documented every three months in 25,000 words. The purpose of starting the diary was to track the progression of PD and to provide an emotional outlet where I could freely express my hopes and fears without upsetting anyone. Sometimes I was defiant and determined to beat each new challenge it threw at me; at other times I felt pathetic and powerless. At this early stage, I experienced three dominant emotions:

Grief - I regretted the passing of an era and the loss of my original identity.

Anger - Why me and why now? I resented having this condition in my forties.
Anxiety - How soon would I have to give up work or stop driving? No-one could answer this.

Diary entry for June 2001

"Anxiety rules my day; it simmers just below the surface and sets off my tremor at the slightest provocation - checking out at the supermarket, speaking in meetings, walking in a crowded corridor - Panic takes hold, tightens its grip and devours my confidence."

Diary entry for May 7th 2003
"This is reality:
I am beginning to lose my identity, vitality and self-confidence. I begin each day with apprehension. My body is out of control and unpredictable. I am losing my drive because there seems no point in striving to improve, innovate or to grow. There is no cure and nothing has changed since I was diagnosed. The world moves on and I trail behind, tripping searching for a refuge out of public view".

But things improved as I read further. Appropriate medication, knowledge and experience enabled me to cope with PD's gradual progression and adapt to the arrival of new symptoms. I would devise some quirky strategy to beat them. I would prepare to go out 30 minutes earlier than usual to avoid rushing and stumbling, have all tickets and cash in easily accessible zipped pockets on a journey.

The anger and grief that blighted my early years with PD faded away as I realised that I could accommodate this condition and that lost skills were replaceable. I temporarily gave up singing, but took up photography at last. More importantly, I began to be less self-centred and to accept that my symptoms were not yet debilitating and my prognosis hopeful. My situation was brought into sharp perspective when two very close friends died in 2005. These were shocking events and I began to ask myself - Why not me?

Anxiety was gradually overcome through the assistance of a counsellor who gave me the chance to unburden my emotions and to analyse the circumstances which provoked panic. I finally cracked the supermarket check-out problem with the help of my youngest son. When I was feeling "off my trolley" and heading for the exit in a state of panic, he managed persuade me to check through just a couple of items. He reassured me that my tremor was not obvious and no-one cared. He managed to reverse the tight cycle of anxiety that had built up over several years.

The turning point came after about 5 years from diagnosis when gradually I moved on from an attitude of resentment to one of acceptance. I would rather not have PD, but there is no point in regretting where I might have been now without it. Although PD has been a challenge and often a trial, it has given me opportunities to meet some remarkable people here where I live, but also at Glasgow where I attended the World Parkinson's Congress in 2010.

These diaries are a convincing record of changing attitudes from anger and anxiety to the realisation that, in the grand scheme of things, I have been fortunate.

2 REVIEW

This chapter focuses on the diagnosis: the gradual emergence of specific symptoms and their identity. Diagnosis of a chronic and progressive disease is a shock, but for those under 50 it can be devastating.

Chapter 3
Telling others

Introduction:
Telling the rest of the world that you now have Parkinson's can be as difficult as finding it out yourself. It is emotionally demanding both to give and to get bad news. Here I'll run through what worked for me, and what to expect in how people will react. Something like 'my gran died of that' can be well-meant but can come across as inconsiderate.

3.1 Responses and reactions
Deciding whom you should inform about your PD diagnosis and how is difficult. Also, you may not feel ready to tell anyone for a while.

Family and close friends
It is likely that you will tell your immediate family or a close friend first. They may well be shocked by this unexpected news. On the one hand, they are coping with your emotions such as grief, anxiety and great uncertainty and they are also coping with their own worries about your needs. They will feel anxious and stressed like you.

Children may not be receptive to an explanation of the complex nature of the disease. Instead, you should try to emphasise that life will not change in the immediate future. For example, if they are still school age, your support as parent, breadwinner, chauffeur and cook (plus other roles) will still be important. With grown-up children, telling them you have PD can be traumatic, especially if they are given the realities straight away. You will find this hard but, in the long term, it will clarify your position, and make them aware of what lies ahead. For example, you may no longer be able to provide financial support.

Your siblings are more likely to accept the news and to offer the right kind of support. However, some may now be concerned that they too may be vulnerable to this condition (although the genetic connection with PD is not proven).

If PD has struck you at a particularly young age, the older generation, such as your parents, may be upset by this worrying news. They may also have friends with PD who have not benefited from the same medical advances that you will receive and you should therefore emphasise your relative advantage in terms of prognosis.

Employers
Having told your immediate family the bad news, you will probably wait a little while before telling your employer (if you have one). Some PWP delay this even for years in the hope that they will not be disadvantaged. If your job involves much physical work or emotional strain and you feel unable to meet its demands, you will need to tell your employer sooner rather than later. Eventually, your PD symptoms will become obvious to your employers and you may have to explain them anyway. Most employers are aware of their responsibilities to their employees and will support them willingly. For example, allowing part-time work or workplace improvements such as providing adaptations to their computer or keyboard or voice recognition.

Of course, telling people is just the first stage of living with PD. As the disease progresses, members of your family and also your close friends may notice the decline. There are times when you may wish to remind them that you are still the same person and you still have the same aspirations and hopes.

Responses on receiving your news

Family, friends, acquaintances and employers will not find it easy to receive your bad news. It all depends upon how you deliver it. If you choose to be pessimistic, they are likely to give you a pessimistic reply. Time and place also matter and ideally, you should choose a time when they are not distracted.

You:
"I have just been diagnosed with Parkinson's"
Possible replies:
"My gran died of that"
"Well, you're lucky it's not cancer"
"That means you just get a bit shaky, doesn't it?"
"Don't worry, there are pills you can take"
"Look at it this way, we all have to die of something."
"Oh well, I'm sure there's a cure just around the corner."
"I've been watching you over the last few months. I knew all along that you had PD".
The recipient gives you a hug with no comment.

3.2 Blog: I'm OK, Thanks by Briony Cooke

Receiving a diagnosis of a long-term illness such as PD can be traumatic, but telling people your bad news may be just as hard. I was reminded of this dilemma by a recently diagnosed friend who was worrying about whom to tell or whether to keep it entirely to himself. Until this recent conversation I had forgotten the trauma of both giving and receiving such news.

Outside my immediate family, I preferred telling people in writing because it allowed them to absorb the idea and respond when and how they felt like it. In 2000 we composed the alternative Xmas letter which focussed on our chronic diseases, poor employment prospects and general misery. In the end, decided not to post this

*self-indulgent testimony. There was no point in spreading our grief.
Phone calls were difficult because facial and vocal responses were missing and telling people face-to-face was nerve racking for me when there was so much emotion involved. There really wasn't an ideal place or time; it was an uncomfortable duty. But this was not simply a one-way process. The recipient had to think on their feet as to how they might respond positively to avoid demoralising me further. But the reality was that few had any idea of the implications of getting PD when relatively young. A very common response from them was to reassure me with the latest bit of research they had read about, usually involving stem cells. In other words, they tried to soften the blow and to boost my morale at the same time.*

Those early days of giving bad news were hard because I was so uncertain myself as to the outcome and how I would be in the future. As time went on, I gradually acquired more and more knowledge and confidence about PD. Despite it, I managed to work for six years and I gained a great deal of satisfaction out of my retirement. Had I known this in those early days I could have been much more positive in delivering my bad news.

If I analyse why I have needed to tell people about my condition, the reasons have changed over time. Initially, when I was still in shock and feeling vulnerable, it was to seek sympathy and support. I also felt I needed to remove all suspicion that my tremor was a result of neurosis or heavy drinking. In those early days, it was a form of apology as to why I was not performing as well as I should. But my attitude has changed and I find myself telling people what I have achieved despite having PD.

I have diverted my attention away from PD during the last few years through creative activities such as writing and photography. These have absorbed my interest and provided much satisfaction and ironically PD has allowed me the time to develop these hobbies through early retirement. For a few years I was immersed in self-pity and had grave doubts about the future, but I am now much more optimistic and have regained my old identity and with that, enthusiasm for life.

It has now become a long-established fact that I have PD and it is accepted by my family and friends as a way of life; a permanent back-drop to all my activities which no longer requires comment. When my medication is working well, I too can put PD to the back of my mind and become myself again instead of that "Person with PD".

In fact, when meeting friends who enquire how I am, my answer is always "I'm OK thanks, and how are you?" There is little point in complaining about symptoms – bradykinesia, dystonia and the rest - because they need explanation and all they wanted to know is that I am OK. Besides, nowadays, I find many of my contemporaries have their own health problems, some of which are much more serious than mine.

3.3 Blog: Accommodating Parkinson's by Briony Cooke

A diagnosis of PD raised all sorts of questions about the future. How long would I be able to work? How would we pay the mortgage if I took early retirement? There was so much uncertainty. But my PD progressed more slowly than expected and I continued to work which enabled us to stay on and improve my entitlement to a pension.

In 1998, two years before my PD diagnosis, we moved to 4-storey house which was in easy reach of the station and a busy town centre. Access to our schools and work were important and the location seemed ideal and we could put down our roots and stay here for years – so I thought.

Then, I was alone in the house one Wednesday afternoon when I found myself frozen at the top of the top flight of stairs, unable to move. This was a sudden "off" period and I could not reach my medication. All I could see was the terrifying stair-well from top to bottom and a flimsy banister in between. Eventually, I crawled to the stairs then descended cautiously on my behind. When I reached the safety of the bedroom below I felt quite drained by the experience. This was something entirely unexpected, but it was a sharp reminder of my frailty. I now take the precaution of avoiding the top floor when my medication is wearing off. This incident made us realise that this "ideal home" had limitations and we needed to consider our options.

We might adapt our house to accommodate my PD, but a series of stair lifts on this winding and fragile staircase would be unsafe and a lift shaft built up the side of the house would contravene building regulations in this conservation area.

The second option is to move out of this house, but stay within the same locality. This would be acceptable, but we are unlikely to match this setting elsewhere in town.

The third option is to move away and find a bungalow in a semi-rural setting where the risks of falling would be minimal. Our two cats could roam freely away from the traffic, I could pursue my gardening interests and my husband could still commute to London. This sounds idyllic, but I worry about social isolation which might be a problem in a village.

Like the passing of time, PD waits for no man (nor woman). If changes in lifestyle need to be made, then there is no time like the present and we shall move reluctantly, but before it becomes an ordeal. It's decision time for us.

3 REVIEW

This chapter deals with your response to the diagnosis in terms of what you say to others and how you react and accommodate the condition.
Resistance or acceptance are extremes in approach, either way, you will need to think about the future and how you will manage.

Key questions
Discuss the advantages and disadvantages of telling people that you have PD soon after diagnosis.
Analyse the responses to your news above and suggest more positive ones.

Chapter 4
Facts and myths; what PD is and is not.

Introduction:
Michael J. Fox has done a wonderful job of raising public awareness of Parkinson's – that it doesn't just affect old people, and that it's still possible to be articulate and funny and engaging even as a long-time sufferer. However, there are many myths that still persist – here I'll try to correct a few of them.

4.1 What is Parkinson's Disease (PD)?
PD is a progressive, chronic (long-term) brain condition that results from the loss of cells in a region of the brain that controls movement (the substantia nigra). This loss causes a deficiency of a certain brain chemical (dopamine) which acts as a neurotransmitter sending messages between the brain and nervous system. Shortage of dopamine causes slow and abnormal movements.

Even though there are many theories as to why these brain cells die, no actual cause of PD has ever been substantiated. However, research has revealed certain risk factors which are discussed below. Treatment typically involves medication to control the symptoms. This can be achieved for some years, but as the disease advances, the medication works less well.

A brief history of treatment
The disease was first recognised as a medical condition – "Paralysis agitans" in 1817 by James Parkinson who published his well-known work "An essay on the shaking palsy".

World PD Day celebrated his birthday April 11, 2017 and 200 years have passed since the essay was published.

James Parkinson was more than a doctor of medicine, he was also a social reformer and political activist.
Since his work was recognised, the only significant progress in developing treatment has been the introduction and universal treatment with Levodopa from 1968. Other medication has been introduced to extend the life of Levodopa and to reduce its side effects.
There is currently no cure for PD.

4.2 What are the risk factors?
Environmental factors – the incidence of PD is higher in urban populations and petrochemicals are a possible cause.
Occupation – studies have shown* that certain occupations are linked to PD. For example, school teachers and medics are vulnerable due to their exposure to infections. Other workers close to or in direct contact with petrochemicals, horticultural or agricultural pesticides have also become more vulnerable. Artists have the lowest incidence of PD.
Genetic factors – a tendency for members of the same family to develop this disease.
Normal age-related process – neuro degeneration is a natural part of ageing, although this is earlier and at a faster rate for a PWP.

PWPs (author included) who neither smoke tobacco nor drink coffee have a greater risk of developing PD.
* http://viartis.net/parkinsons.disease/prevalence.htm

4.3 Prevalence
Prevalence is the number of people in an area or country who have PD per 100,000 population. In the UK the prevalence is currently 150 per 100,000.

There are very approximately 10 million people in the world who have PD. However, the reliability of the statistics is in question because of the inconsistencies in the definition of PD and the methods of data collection and processing.

PD is the second most common chronic neurodegenerative condition in older people especially beyond the age of 60. This means that in regions such as North America and Europe prevalence is high because the population structure is ageing and there is a high % of people over 60. The area with the lowest current prevalence is Ethiopia with only 7 per 100,000. In a less economically developed country such as this, the population structure is young and the % of population over 60 is small. The cause of death in Ethiopia is more likely to be an infectious disease than PD.

PD can appear at any age, but the average age of onset worldwide is 60. PD is rare in people younger than 30, and risk for the disease increases with age. It is estimated that 5–10% of patients who have PD experience symptoms before the age of 40. PD is common in the elderly and affects one person in 20 over the age of 80. The gender balance favours men slightly more than women.

4.4 Common myths:
Life expectancy of PWP is the same as that of the population without PD.
True, but the quality of life for those with PD is generally poor.

Tremor is the principal symptom of PD.
Untrue. Less than 30% are tremor dominant and other important symptoms may be poor balance and slowness of movement.

Pain is not a regular feature of PD.
Untrue. For some PWP it is a major problem particularly when their medication wears off.

You do not die of PD.
Untrue. You may die of pneumonia or choking both of which are problematic symptoms of advanced PD. The cause of death on a death certificate may underplay the role of PD.

PD is an old man's disease
Untrue. Although worldwide there are 1.2 men for every woman diagnosed, they are not all old. 5-10% of newly diagnosed patients are younger than 40.

The symptoms of PD
The drawing below shows a PWP with advanced disease. These symptoms can be lessened significantly by medication especially in the early years.

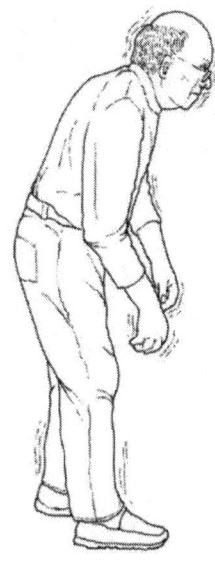

Postural instability (poor balance) leads to stooping and shuffling as the patient strives to stay upright.

Gait is usually rapid and arm-swing slight.

Tremor often starts in the hands, but can also be felt internally and can affect the head and the limbs. There are two sorts – a resting tremor and an action tremor. A Parkinson's tremor is relatively slow with a speed of 3 cycles per second.

Fig. 3 –PD posture. Source: Jane Upton.

4.5 Raising awareness
Blog: Shaking out the misconceptions by Briony Cooke
About five years ago I was in town and came face-to-face with a student whom I had taught over 15 years earlier. I remembered him as a likeable plodder and he remembered me as very pushy, but entertaining. That was a compliment indeed, but when he asked about how my work was going, I had to tell him about my ill-health retirement because of PD. He was surprised and said he would never have guessed. That made my day, but later I reflected how he had seen me at my best and how his impression might have been very different had seen me with my medication wearing off. These fluctuations make our condition quite variable and deceptive and it's no wonder that the public can't get the measure of this illness and might underestimate its impact on us. I wanted to see how PD was widely perceived and searched the Internet for images of PD symptoms. Of the first 20 images, 13 were of elderly men shuffling or trembling, three of a hand trembling and the rest showed various neurological symptoms. Presumably, these images portray the most common perception of PD. Statistically, this is correct and the global PD population is over 60 with more males than females and many experiencing tremor. Nevertheless, there are also a significant number of us with young onset PD diagnosed under 50 and our experience of living with PD is quite different from that of the patient with later onset; we may have jobs to maintain, financial pressures and families to support.

There is a lot more to PD than its visible symptoms such as tremor. For me, non-motor symptoms such as insomnia, internal tremor, digestive problems, pain, muscle weakness and low blood pressure are more troublesome. Many of these symptoms are invisible and therefore unrecognised or disregarded. We cannot blame the public for their lack of knowledge so long as we go on hiding away our worst symptoms and only appearing at our best.

This is the dilemma we have to overcome.

Many of us try to disguise our visible symptoms such as tremor or poor balance because they may give the false impression that we are either very nervous or even drunk. I have been the focus of funny looks several times when I have been "off" and only leave home when my medication is working well, usually one hour after taking my pills. In the early days, before I was on medication my tremor was dominant and I used to hide it by stuffing my left hand in the pocket of my jacket while teaching. Better understanding and knowledge of the condition would help to avoid this embarrassment.

April 11–17th was PD awareness week here in the UK. Every year, it is an opportunity for those of us living with PD to educate the public about the nature of our disease, how it affects our quality of life and the particular disadvantages of those diagnosed at a young age. This is our window of opportunity when we can change attitudes and raise the profile of this disease which is undramatic, but nevertheless debilitating in the long-term.

During this week, Kathie Smallwood, a fellow member of our young onset support group, spoke out on local radio for a good half-hour enlightening the presenter and public about day-to-day living with PD and the problems of public misconception. She cleverly conveyed the message that PD is a challenge and distressing at times, but a positive attitude and a sense of humour can make it tolerable. She copes by looking after herself by taking regular physical exercise through Pilates and hydrotherapy. When asked about her future, she said philosophically that there was no point in worrying about those things over which she had no control. Her message was convincing and genuine and went a long way in raising public awareness

By educating the public in this way we are also drawing attention to our funding needs and the urgency of finding a cure for PD.

4 REVIEW

This chapter raises the important question of public perception of PD. Unfortunately, searching the internet reveals some disturbing revelations which we must change: Old men get PD and its main symptom is tremor. This is wrong.
PD affects young people (including women), it is a serious and debilitating condition. People stay at home when the condition advances which reduces public awareness of the suffering it causes.

Key question
Examine the factors that affect the level of funding for medical research. Compare annual research expenditure for PD, cancer, Alzheimer's. (Refer to the annual accounts of specific charities). Draw conclusions.

Chapter 5
Taking control

Introduction: In this chapter, I'll run through regular Parkinson's medication, along with their pros and cons. I will also give you some tips about food to eat or to avoid.
This chapter contains the key facts. Some of these may be quite unfamiliar. Do not be concerned if the concepts seem complex. For example, you don't need to be able to explain the interaction between Levodopa and protein, but just to avoid the consequences.

Your medication regime is determined by your doctor or PD nurse, but there are other ways of optimising treatment which you do yourself. Physical exercise will keep you reasonably fit and socialising provides support.

Being in control means that you make informed decisions and that you feel in charge of your condition. It does not mean that you are solely responsible and you will not need the advice of the medical professionals from time to time. They will devise a medication routine for you to follow and then periodically you will give them feedback.
Managing other aspects of your life such as exercise, diet and socialising will be your responsibility. This is self-help and it just as important as the medication.

5.1 Medication - Managing Levodopa (L-Dopa)
Levodopa is the most effective drug for the treatment of slowness of movement (bradykinesia), tremor and rigidity, but balance (postural instability) and coordination are less likely to improve. Names of drugs shown below are those used in the UK; they vary in other countries.

In all forms, taken as a pill, Levodopa is combined in various concentrations with another compound (Carbidopa) to improve its efficiency and reduce side effects. Carbidopa alone has no benefit. In the UK, Carbidopa-Levodopa is called Sinemet. Carbidopa-Levodopa is available in three different quick-acting formulations: 10/100 (Sinemet plus), 25/100, and 25/250 (the numerator is the Carbidopa dose in milligrams and the denominator is the Levodopa dose). Two slow-release formulations are available: Controlled release Carbidopa-Levodopa (or CR Sinemet) 25/100 and 50/20.

In Europe, Levodopa is combined with Benserazide (Madopar). As PD advances, it may become necessary to add Entacapone to Levodopa to prolong its action somewhat. These pills are called Stalevo.

Many people take prolonged release tablets to give a 24-hour background boost to the Levodopa. These pills such as Mirapexin (Pramipexole) may be introduced by physicians before Levodopa. Many patients find that dispersible Madopar is absorbed very quickly and can delay or reduce the severity an "off" period.

Dose — Most patients in the UK usually start treatment with a small dose of Sinemet or Madopar (62.5 mg). The dose is then slowly increased over several days, depending on the person's tolerance, to the lowest dose that controls symptoms. This is known as the maintenance dose.

Side effects — The most common side effects of Levodopa are nausea, sleepiness, dizziness, and headache. More serious side effects can include confusion, hallucinations, delusions, agitation, and psychosis. These are more common in older people. Side effects can usually be avoided or minimized by starting with a low dose and increasing it gradually. This is known as titration.

5.2 Complications of Levodopa
The "On" and "Off" syndrome

After patients have been taking Levodopa for a number of years they may start to experience the "on / off" syndrome. This is a regular cycle of the "on" and "off" states that corresponds to the intake of Levodopa,

The "on" state occurs about 45 minutes after the dose. It varies between individuals and can also be controlled by the amount of food in the gut (jejunum). The "on" state, which eliminates most of the Parkinson's symptoms, may be regarded as a relief, but the response to Levodopa in more advanced PWP may be extreme. These patients may experience dyskinesia which are involuntary movements affecting many parts of the body. Some people dread the occurrence of dyskinesia because they are associated with lack of control. It is true to say that the "off" state when the PD symptoms of tremor, stiffness, poor balance and weakness return is universally hated.

This roller-coaster of ups and downs typifies PD after a number of years.

5.3 Blog: The roller-coaster ride by Briony Cooke

The on/off syndrome began to appear very gradually about ten years after diagnosis; my medication became less effective after about 3 hours, but the next pill did not kick in until another hour. This meant that in the course of a 15 hour day, I would lose about 6 hours when I was quite helpless and my symptoms would be at full-throttle. At these "off" times, I would not wish to be out and about because my walking and balance were poor. When the medication finally kicked in, I would feel fine and start to function normally. I think this is the most difficult aspect of this disease. Its fluctuating nature means that some people may find it unconvincing. For example, you may emerge from a car, exhibiting a Blue Badge* looking perfectly normal and your eligibility may be questioned by another driver or passer-by. You *may need to be prepared for this kind of antagonism. There are several possible responses:*

You can ask them whether they would like to have your disease or you can just walk away. If you engage in argument, you are likely to induce symptoms which are convincing on the one hand, but demoralising for you on the other.

At peak dose, I experience dyskinesia. It is quite easy to spot this dyskinetic phase with me. I call it my "motor-mouth" phase. My symptoms can include non-stop repetitive singing of 60s hits like "I've lost that loving feeling" by the Righteous Brothers and at the other end of the scale bits of the Hallelujah Chorus. Endless drivel includes talking to the pets (cats and tortoises) about the current political crisis. My mood becomes over-enthusiastic and in public places I become extremely sociable and start to offer old ladies a hand as we get off the bus. I am in a state of over-activity, but I prefer this to the nagging pain of being "off".

I enter a phase of normality for about an hour and am no longer a public embarrassment. During this stable phase, I do most of my useful work; typing, cooking and general domesticating. Then gradually, the PD symptoms return as the medication wears off and the cycle starts all over again. This is my roller-coaster of a day.

The on-off syndrome was one of the symptoms that the brain stimulation can reduce. This means that I now have a background of stimulation derived from my pacemaker which evens out the ups and down.

*A Blue Badge is a parking permit issued to people with mobility problems in the UK.

5.4 Managing protein with Levodopa

PWP who take Levodopa often find that their medication (Sinemet, Madopar and Stalevo) is less effective if they eat protein-rich foods soon after taking it or they take Levodopa after a large protein-rich meal. The reason for this is complex, but involves competition between L-Dopa and amino acids (from protein) at the absorption sites. These are at the blood-brain barrier and the small bowel (jejunum). If the protein is in a large quantity, it can suppress the absorption of your next dose of medication. If you find that you are sensitive to protein you should avoid protein-rich foods during the day and ensure that your stomach is empty when you take your next dose of medication. If you decide to have protein at any time of day, you should be cautious and follow the following schedule:

Recommended lunch-time / medication schedule.
12 00 Take Levodopa medication as prescribed.

Wait 45 minutes before eating protein rich food.

Wait 2 hours before taking the next dose of Levodopa medication, if possible. This will allow sufficient time for the protein to be digested

Ideally, the consumption of protein should be delayed until the last meal of the day because it will not matter that your PD symptoms return during the night. Your doctor may prescribe prolonged release Levodopa which should ensure that you are reasonably comfortable during the night.

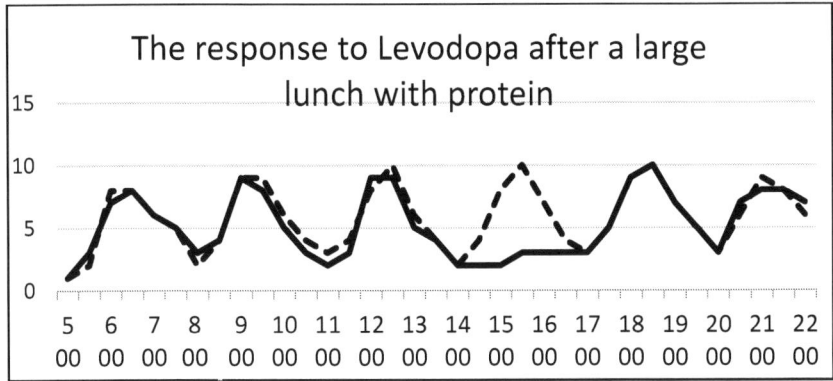

Fig. 4

Dotted line - Normal response to 3 hourly doses of Levodopa starting at 05 00 and ending at 21 00.

Note that each dose peaks between 1 and 1.5 hours later.

Solid line – This shows an adverse response around 15 00 after a protein-rich lunch.

The response scores (shown in the left axis) are subjective and represent how the on/off states feel to the PWP.

Interpretation - 10 = excellent and 1 = poor.

Question The table below shows 4 different types of food and their protein content.
For each of these 4 types, calculate the average % protein content and identify the type of food which is best avoided at lunch-time. Explain how and why some PWP control their daily protein intake.

Dairy	%	**Fish**	%	**Meat**	%	**Vegetables**	%
Edam	25	Salmon	22	Lamb	35	Nuts	23
Ricotta	12	Lobster	16	Chicken	25	Lentils	29
Parmesan	40	Cod	15	Beef	25	Potato chips	4
Feta	14	Scallops	14	Turkey	25	Peas	4
Average		Average		Average		Average	

Recommended daily diet for a PWP taking Levodopa
(e.g. Sinemet, Madopar, Stalevo).

Breakfast
Poached or boiled egg with tomatoes and mushrooms
Prunes or natural yoghurt, two tablespoons of golden linseed

Lunch
Fruit juice (not grapefruit) or vegetable soup (squash, celery, leek, carrot)
Jacket potato, rice or pasta with vegetables

Dinner
Fish, chicken or egg.
Leafy vegetables such as broccoli or cabbage.
Fruit salad.

Each meal is taken after Levodopa has taken effect
Drink at least 8-9 cups of fluid per day, preferably tap or mineral water.

This diet is low on fats and refined sugar. It is delicious and nutritious and includes a wide variety of minerals. It just shows the types of food you can choose, but you can ring the changes from day to day.
There is no need to buy any expensive foods and ready meals can save time and effort, but check their ingredients and sell-by dates.
In the case of your being underweight or overweight, it is best to consult your GP or your consultant who is most likely to refer you to a dietician.

5.5 Other medication

Monoamine Oxidase B (MAO B) inhibitors. These work by blocking the effect of enzymes that inactivate dopamine. They have been given to patients because they can modestly reduce symptoms of PD and were once thought to be neuroprotective. Neurologists once prescribed these pills to be taken once daily, but the limited benefits were often cancelled by side-effects such as nausea, headache, and difficulty falling asleep.

Dopamine agonists. Dopamine agonists work by directly stimulating dopamine receptors in the brain. Those in regular use in the UK include Mirapexin (Pramipexole) and Requip (Ropinirole).

When deciding which medication to use initially, patients and clinicians must consider the potential benefits of dopamine agonists (fewer Levodopa-related motor complications if Levodopa can be delayed) as well as the risks (possibly less effective control of PD symptoms and more side effects). Age also plays a part: if the patient is young (under 50) and is likely to need medication for several decades, it is best to delay Levodopa to avoid a situation where the options decrease.

Dosing — Dopamine agonists are taken by mouth daily or by skin patch. The oral treatment may be taken three times daily or in prolonged relief form, one pill per day.

Side effects — Clinical trials have found that dopamine agonists are effective in controlling the symptoms of PD, but less effective than Levodopa. They may have serious side effects such as swelling of the legs, visual hallucinations, and OCDs (Obsessive Compulsive Disorders). These disorders might include hypersexuality, compulsive gambling, eating and shopping. Starting with a low dose and increasing slowly over a period of several weeks may help to minimize side effects.

COMT Inhibitors. The most common Catechol-O-Methyl Transferase (COMT) inhibitors used in the UK is Entacapone. It is used for people with motor fluctuations who have "wearing off" periods at the end of their dose of Levodopa.
Dosing — Entacapone may be combined with Levodopa as Stalevo or taken separately.
Side effects — The most common side effects of Entacapone include dyskinesia, hallucinations, confusion, nausea, orange discoloration of the urine and low blood pressure after standing up.

Amantadine. Amantadine is an antiviral drug that was originally developed to prevent influenza but was found to improve mild symptoms (tremor, akinesia – lack of movement - and rigidity) in people with PD. It is also thought to reduce dyskinesia in people with advanced disease. Amantadine is usually taken by mouth two to three times per day.
Side effects — Possible side effects of Amantadine include visual hallucinations and confusion, livedo reticularis (blotchy, purple-coloured areas of skin, usually found on the wrists and legs), and swelling of the ankles.

5.6 Treatment of non-motor symptoms
PD is a movement disorder and the medication described above is designed to treat its motor symptoms. Non-motor symptoms are also typical of PD, but seldom fully recognised. For some PWP non-motor symptoms are dominant and more difficult to control.

Mood disorders
Depression and anxiety are the most common mental health problems experienced by people with PD. (See chapter 8).
A class of medication called SSRIs (selective serotonin reuptake inhibitors) is commonly used with some success.

Sleep disorders — Somnolence (daytime sleepiness) and insomnia (difficulty sleeping at night) and daytime fatigue are frequent problems for people with PD, and are often a result of night-time sleeping problems such as frequent awakening. Treatment options include improving sleep habits, recognising and treating problems that disrupt sleep at night (such as difficulty turning or changing position in bed, pain, and the need to urinate frequently). The use of a stimulant (such as caffeine) to decrease sleepiness during the day may sometimes be helpful. See **Chapter 9** for more details on sleep.

Dementia — Cognitive changes such as problems with attention span, task execution, planning, language and memory are common among people with PD, especially as the disease progresses and the PWP ages. A class of medications known as cholinesterase inhibitors, which were originally developed to treat Alzheimer's disease, may help to improve these symptoms.

Psychosis and hallucinations — The treatment of psychosis and hallucinations in people with PD often includes stopping or decreasing the dose of one or more of the medications used to treat the motor symptoms of PD.

Orthostatic hypotension - a drop in blood pressure and light-headedness when standing.

Other non-motor symptoms
These are listed below and most are treatable:
Slow gastric motility often associated with gastric reflux and constipation
Pain and fatigue
Excessive sweating
Seborrheic dermatitis or an oily skin
Urinary urgency and incontinence

Loss of sense of smell
Sexual problems
Weight loss
Speech and swallowing problems.

5.7 Digestion and diet
Gastric (stomach) reflux
The digestive system of PWP is far from efficient. Motility (movement) of food through the gut becomes progressively slower as the condition advances. Acid reflux (regurgitation of acids and food from the oesophagus and stomach) is commonly associated with PD and is difficult to treat. Due to swallowing difficulties, surgery to prevent the reflux if not usually feasible.

Constipation
Another problem that is almost universal with PD is constipation. This is also caused by low gut motility, but also several of the dopaminergic drugs including Levodopa which slow down activity in all parts of the digestive system.
Constipation is serious because, as well as causing distress to PWP, it can make dopaminergic drugs more difficult to absorb and therefore less effective.

Diet in general
The advice given to the PWP is the same as to the population as a whole. Healthy eating is recommended and this means a mixed diet containing:
Vegetables, fruit, (vitamins and roughage)
Proteins (milk, eggs, cheese, fish, nuts, meat)
Fats in moderation
Sugars in moderation and non-refined.

Specific remedies for constipation include:
Golden linseed (2 table spoons per day sprinkled on cereal)

Stone fruit (plums, prunes, cherries and apricots)
Plenty of water to maintain hydration and avoid constipation (8-9 cups per day).

5.8 The importance of exercise.
Exercise is important for all, but PWP have several physical limitations which exercise can improve:
Balance
Muscle strength
Joint flexibility
Stamina
Lethargy

In the UK, many local support groups run by volunteers and supported by Parkinson's UK have a range of different types of exercise classes. They vary in terms of focus and they are designed to suit people at different stages of disease advancement. There is no reason why you should not find a class to suit you.

Tai chi is a form of gentle exercise but nevertheless very disciplined which focuses upon muscle strength, balance and joint flexibility.

Pilates is very popular but it's important that you join a class developed particularly for PWP. This requires more input from you and is designed to work on all parts of the body and to strengthen your core muscles. The exercises can be done on the floor and you use various inflatables to improve your balance.

Hydrotherapy is probably one of the most beneficial of these types of exercises. It can be a successful therapy for those PWP with more advanced disease. Of course, there needs to be a suitable pool and physiotherapist in your district. This is often a problem in the UK and you will be very lucky to find one near you. Hydrotherapy involves exercise in water where its buoyancy supports you. If you have difficulty with getting into the pool there may well be a hoist available, but you would need to check these things out first.

Exercise is not just physically beneficial but also socially worthwhile and many people enjoy these classes because of making friends and having good chat.
In the UK, these classes are often subsidised by the local Parkinson's support group or the local authority. Usually, this makes them accessible to most people although cost is a feature that deters some. The other problem is access; getting to and from exercise classes may be a problem for those who are less mobile.

Fig. 5 A hydrotherapy session at the Royal Berks Hospital, Reading.
Photo by permission of PEPS and RBH.

5.9 Blog: Support Groups by Briony Cooke

When I retired in 2006 I decided I would investigate the local Parkinson's support group. I went to a church hall to one of the meetings in August. It was packed out because the speaker was my consultant neurologist. I understood that he came every year to tell us about the latest happenings in the PD world. He was an engaging speaker; a bit of a showman. After about an hour there was a tea break. It was then that I turned and looked around and saw advanced cases of PD. I was shocked and stunned to imagine that everyone ended up in a wheelchair - or so it appeared. I tried not to look shocked, but it was quite horrifying. I would not return and there was no way I was going to end up dribbling in a wheelchair like them. I rushed away from the meeting vowed that I would never return. Looking back, I realise that my response was very uncaring and irrational.

I wanted to meet people who had PD but not at the advanced stage. I got in touch with PD UK and I asked them how easy it was to set up a young onset group. The outcome was that myself and another PWP set up a local group for people with young onset PD. That was in 2007. The group consisted then of about 16 PWP plus their partners most of them between the ages of 40 and 60 and the majority of whom were still at work. Socially, it was a success. We organised all sorts of activities including therapies such as hydrotherapy and Pilates, curry nights in and dinners out. Eventually, the numbers dwindled when access to meetings became a problem for less mobile members with more advanced PD. Several of these are Asian members who were all active once and made a great cultural contribution to the group. PD has isolated them and this is a significant loss. Sadly, we have also lost six members since 2007: four with an aggressive type of PD and two with conditions unrelated to PD.

Despite these setbacks, the group continues to provide advice and friendship which is much valued by its members. In 2017 we celebrated our 10-year anniversary.

The needs of young onset PWP are quite different from those of the older patient:
Many are still in full-time work
Some have family still living at home
Financial commitments are high - mortgages and education costs
They have to live with a chronic disease which has no cure at present
Treatments have to be effective over a long time
Support groups for young onset PWP give them the opportunity to discuss these issues at meetings and to resolve some of them. Members value the social side of these meetings as much as the informative side.
Having a group where all members either have PD or are closely involved with this condition means that we can relax and forget about our symptoms.

5 - REVIEW

Taking control of your PD means accepting and adapting to prescribed medication. Along with this is the business of acquiring sufficient knowledge to manage your condition well and to optimise function; it's not just a matter of popping pills. To make Levodopa work, you must understand how PD affects digestion. What you eat and when and how much you eat are all relevant to a healthy system that keeps moving.

Looking after yourself also involves exercise and socialising. The approach must be holistic (treating several aspects at once).

Key question.
If you were setting up a young onset support group in your area, how would you attract members?

Chapter 6
Other options

Introduction:
This chapter evaluates the other options available to PWP. There are ways of improving our quality of life and those of others in the PD community, but we have to evaluate the risk. Both clinical trials and surgery involve risk, but they both bring hope.
(These long personal accounts are written by Dilys Parker and Briony Cooke and are presented in a Roman font for easier reading).

6.1 Clinical trials
These are experiments or observations done in clinical research. They are designed to answer specific questions about biomedical or behavioural interventions using data collected from the participants involved. In the UK, researchers must first seek the approval of an ethics committee. (Proponents of new drugs, vaccines and devices may seek approval in this way).
Many new drugs have been adopted through this process.

6.2 Blog: Dilys Parker's experience of clinical trials
The most recent trial I volunteered for was also the most demanding. I underwent brain surgery and a year's intensive monitoring followed. Why do I continue to be involved in trials? There are a multitude of motivating factors but there are also some potentially negative effects or outcomes. Here are my Cs which I had to consider before committing myself.

Consider trials in the early days. It is worth checking before you begin medication. Are there any in your area looking for untreated patients? I know of people who have been able to trial new and novel therapies long before they hit the market.

Commitment to following through is important. Do I have the time and the interest in this trial? Equally, if not more significant, is finding out what the researchers and their funders commitment is to you. Do they cover expenses? If the treatment is successful will you be able to continue it at the end of the trial?

Contributing to the greater good can be a motivator. Being in a trial means we are helping in the search for treatments that will improve our lives. Many research projects do not start on time because they struggle to get enough participants. Ultimately, it is those of us with PD whose wellbeing is compromised by time delays.

Community is important for people affected by PD. It is developed through a sense of connection. Professional confidentiality requirements can mean the research experience is solitary, but meeting others with PD occurs in many differing situations. Having a shared research experience can provide a welcome and unexpected link with others.

Care has been a prime a motivator for me to undertake trials. I appreciate the focused attention of Parkinson's experts and time with them. I learn about the condition and my own version of it. Depending on the trial, I am encouraged to become reflective and in the process I learn to identify and monitor factors that contribute to my wellbeing.

Caution is required before agreeing to any trial. Expectations and trial provisions vary. The questions that we ask may be the same but the answers are likely to be quite different depending on the country where you live. Do your homework. You will find much is well documented in the informed consent literature. Consider if the research will ultimately benefit the PD community or will it be just an academic exercise. Find out what happens if there is an adverse event and who pays for research related injuries. How and when will you be informed of outcomes? If you receive the placebo what happens if the results are positive? Will you be offered the treatment and will it be free?

Once upon a time I thought I was bullet-proof, and in control of my world. I had ideas of what I wanted to do with my life and how my future was going to unfold. To have PD rudely intrude was never a part of the plan, but it did. Being involved in clinical trials is a choice. A choice that was offered when it seemed many choices had been modified or taken away. Research trials have been a positive experience for me, I think they are worth considering.

6.3 An introduction to Deep Brain Stimulation by Briony Cooke

Deep Brain Stimulation involves the implantation of two leads or electrodes into the brain. The leads are attached to a pulse generator embedded in the patient's chest and through them electrical charges are delivered to the STN (sub-thalamic nucleus). These charges can reduce or eliminate the confused neurological messages that occur with PD when the neurotransmitter – dopamine – is absent or in short supply. Here are my experiences of DBS.

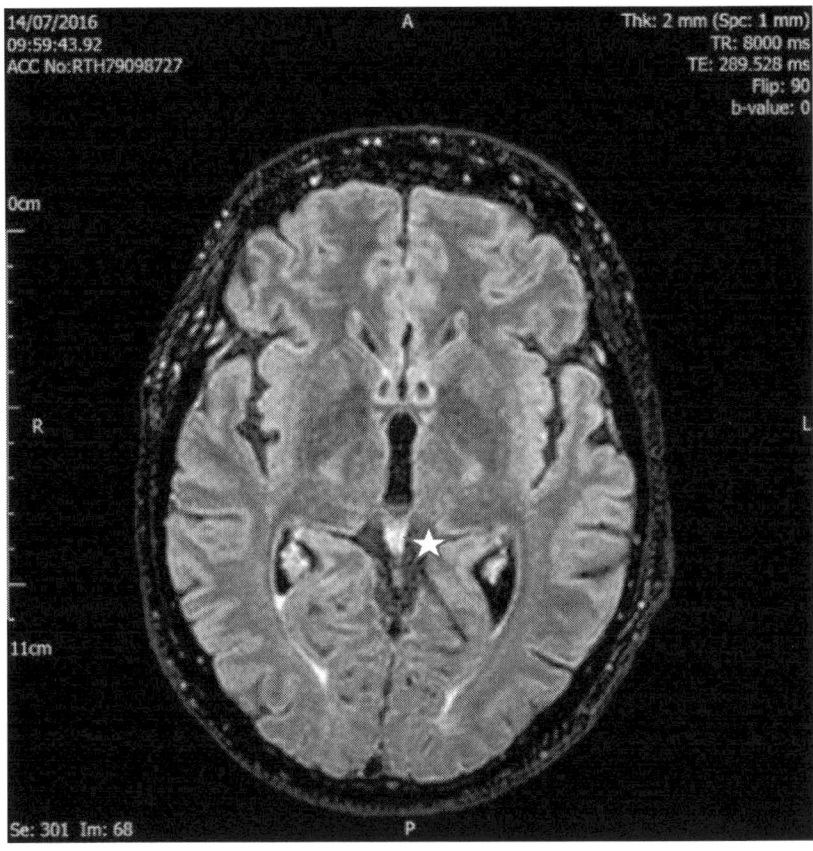

Fig. 6 STN (Sub thalamic nucleus)

This scan of my brain was taken before DBS surgery to locate precisely the STN. The star shows the position of the STN. This was the target for the 2 electrodes which were implanted during the surgery.

Source: John Radcliffe Hospital Oxford

6.4 Blog: Holes in the head by Briony Cooke
September 2013 – DBS, the surgical option

It was in September 2013 that my consultant neurologist at the Royal Berkshire Hospital suggested Deep Brain Stimulation as a surgical treatment that could give me a new lease of life and take me back to where I had been 5-10 years ago. It was not a cure, PD would progress as before, but several of my symptoms would be controlled and my quality of life would improve. At first, I was quite taken aback, because I didn't think that my PD was sufficiently far advanced to be eligible for this type of surgery. Besides, there was the overwhelming deterrent of having the operation done when I was awake; something I couldn't contemplate at this stage. However, when I gave it some thought, I realised my current drug treatment was becoming ever less effective despite increasing the dose. The side effects of Levodopa became progressively worse with usage. The worst was dyskinesia – uncontrollable movements of the limbs and eventually the whole body which made most activities impossible. I already experienced these each evening on my left side, along with a feeling of extreme restlessness and agitation. After much hesitation, I decided have my name added to the DBS waiting list and meanwhile learn about the pros and cons of this procedure.

I was to have the operation at the John Radcliffe Hospital in Oxford, a centre of excellence. I read their handbook on DBS which discussed the procedures, the benefits and the risks involved. I came to the conclusion that it was the only way out of my predicament. I had given up on there being a cure for PD within my lifetime; to depend on this would only lead to disappointment and keeping up morale through false hope was no solution. I had learnt to be realistic when it came to the "cure" and there was no time to lose.

But it was not that easy and at three in the morning when I lay awake dwelling on the negative aspects of DBS; the risk of a brain haemorrhage during the operation, post-operative infection and psychological changes. These were genuine risks and more likely than previous surgical procedures I had experienced: correction of short-sightedness when I was nine, numerous obstetric interventions, four endoscopies and a couple of bunion jobs. All these seemed quite trivial. There are few operations that catch the attention of the listener more than "brain surgery". It has a terrifying mystique and can kill a conversation dead. For example, on the afternoon before my admission I went down to the village hardware shop and on leaving I said:
"I won't see you for a bit because I'll be in hospital."
"Oh dear. Nothing serious, I hope?"
"Well actually, I'm having brain surgery."
"Gosh... well... er... good luck!"
"Can I give you a lift home?"

March 31 2014 - Neuropsychological Tests
Having agreed to go ahead with DBS, I had to undergo a rigorous programme of tests to ensure that I was suitable for this procedure and that the outcome would be successful. At the end of March, I was admitted to the John Radcliffe Hospital as an in-patient. The first morning I had to complete two hours of neuropsychological tests to determine whether I was developing dementia or would not cope emotionally with the operation. The tests had to be done at great speed and put me under considerable pressure, but were not difficult. The first test had me listing all the things beginning with S found in the supermarket. That seemed easy enough but then I had to recite number sequences forwards, backwards and in numerical order with the sequence getting longer every time. These exercises were interspersed with recounting stories and lists which I was asked to repeat several tests later. By the end my mind was totally boggled.

After this stage, I was admitted to the Neuroscience ward. My companions in Room 27 were one opposite who vomited/apologised constantly, the older woman one to my left recovering from cranial surgery and looked depressed. In any other situation where you were going to spend a whole day with a group of individuals each with a dramatic story to tell, you would at least introduce yourself, but I soon realised the social limitations of this situation. It's not done to ask: "Well, what are you in for?"

The lack of privacy makes patients wary of disclosing too much information about themselves. Except in the case of one of my room-mates who loudly shared her mobile phone conversation with us: "Well me tummy's a bit sore coz they had to take some bits of fat and stuff it up my nose to fill the gap."
As an in-patient, I spent the evening imagining how ghastly it was going to be without medication for about 14 hours. My last dose was 21:00; then I would gradually seize up. I placed everything as close as possible to me in bed, but forgot to put the alarm within reach, which meant a long delay before a bed-pan arrived. My dignity dissolved. The night passed painfully slowly.

The assessment team had agreed to come early and put me out of my agony because once their tests were done, I would be able to have my medication. By the time they came, I had to be assisted to sit upright and to stand. They gave me the conventional UPDRS (Unified Parkinson's Disease Rating Scale) test for both my left and my right side and predictably my left side performed very badly. The object of the exercise assisted assessment physical capabilities on both sides to determine whether I needed unilateral or bilateral stimulation of my subthalamic nucleus (STN - the bit in the middle of my brain, the size of a small grain of rice which needed tweaking).

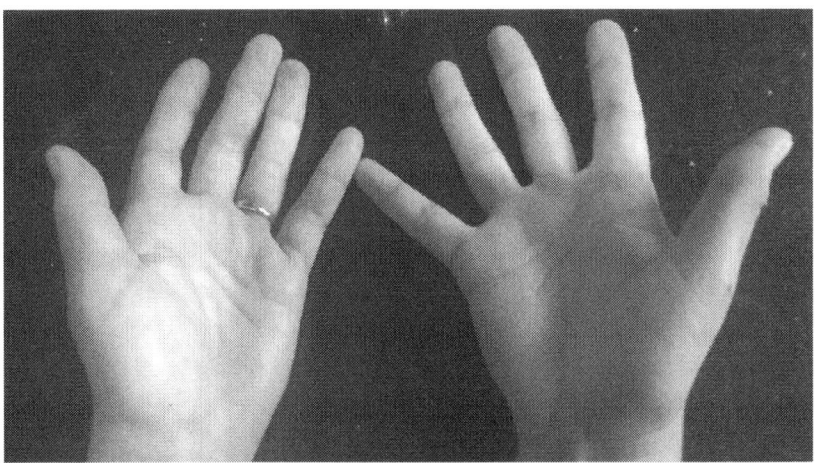

Fig. 7
The author's hands showing weakness in left hand where the muscles are seldom extended due to tightness and pain. There is weakness throughout the left side of the body. Tests using the UPDRS scale reveal that the left side is significantly more symptomatic than the right.

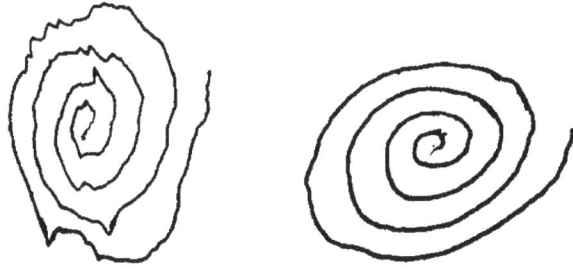

Fig. 8
This is a common test of the relative strength of one hand. It is used in the UDPRS test. (See Glossary).

Being right handed also adds to the contrast between the two hands.

The loss of dignity was compounded by my attire. I am not sure why I had to wear an operation gown to be videoed, but it added nicely to the unattractiveness of my appearance. I hoped sincerely that they meant what they said and the video would not appear on YouTube.

At 11 a.m. I was allowed to take my medication which was a huge relief and then I was reassessed using the same rating scale as before and the change was remarkable. After this I was free to go.

About a month later I received a report sent to my GP with the results of the tests. I was described as "intellectually intact" and with "moderate physical disability". It was like receiving exam results once again. The most significant thing was that my right side was 60% better physically than my left side. Nevertheless, they had decided that they would operate on both sides.
My case was discussed at a panel meeting and it was recommended that I was put forward for surgery. I also had to meet the criteria for funding by the National Health Service, although I still had to attend a day of pre-operative assessment to ensure that I was physically fit for surgery.

Having passed this part of the selection procedure, I had to have an MRI scan of my brain. This took place in the outpatients' department on July 10 where I remained for the day because of having a general anaesthetic.

July 24 2014 – Bad news
I received a phone call from the secretary of the consultant radiologist asking me if "anyone had talked to me about my scan because there was an abnormality". This threw me into a state of panic. This turned out to be an aneurysm in the artery connecting the left and right sides of my brain at the front. It was only 3mm across and the consultant described as "incidental"– this means that they were not looking for it. Such a feature causes problems in 1% of patients and the majority do not know they have an aneurysm. I was particularly concerned that it would delay or cancel my operation, but reassuringly the consultant said it would not, although I would have to have it monitored every six months for the next five years.
It was no fun having the boat rocked at this stage, but the outcome was relief.
It meant that I had my operation date changed from August 6 to 14. Frustrating, but necessary.

I got my bag packed for the hospital about two weeks in advance and spent a long time puzzling over whether I should take my own satin sheets or not in order that I could turnover at night. I fixed up Wi-Fi so that I could play all-night Scrabble with my Parky friends. I took along a couple of books which I thought would be light-hearted and funny. As it turned out I had very little time or inclination to read.

During those last few days I went on several walks around the village and towards the river which I always found inspirational: it was always changing, but always there; something permanent and reliable. The weather was exceptionally warm and shady streets elegantly framed by trees in full leaf. They would still be here when I returned, but I would be changed. I wondered whether I would see the river and walk the streets again, I hoped so. I looked at my beans and peas growing in our garden and thought how next time I saw them they would be ready to eat. I inspected my tortoise eggs which of course were due to hatch the week I was in hospital and my husband the midwife. The event I had been anticipating for a month, I was going to miss.

On the edge of my consciousness there was a persistent and profound worry which I would admit to no-one. Would I get through this surgery? Would I be one of the 3% who suffer a brain haemorrhage? Might I spend the rest of my life in a wheelchair? Or worse. What if I have this operation and the outcome is no improvement. There were a number of Parkies I knew who were too scared to have this procedure done. Maybe my life wasn't that bad and I could cope without surgery? The questions were always there and there were no answers. Henry (my husband) wanted me to go ahead with surgery and I respected his view because he would be responsible for my care in the long-term, I should not underestimate the strength of his feelings. So, I went ahead.

August 13 – Impatient In-patient
I rang the Neuroscience ward as instructed at 12:00 to find out if there was a bed available. There would be a bed at 15:30, if we could get to the hospital ASAP. As it turned out I was not allocated a bed until 18:30 by which time I had missed tea.
I was in a room with two other patients, both had back problems which sounded quite serious. They were pleasant enough except one insisted on having the television on full blast all night. Her successor and mother of three with a benign spinal tumour, was much more amenable. She spent the first night in either in agony when she was not on morphine or throwing up when she was. However, the next day she was much better and we got chatting about children and we ended up singing "California Dreaming'".

Wednesday August 14 – Stage 1 surgery

I was first on the list for surgery on Wednesday the 14th. I watched the clock tick by as it approached 08:30 when they were expected to come and get me. Suddenly, there was a flurry of activity and the boys in blue scrubs turned up to take me to the operating theatre. Earlier that morning I had been visited by the anaesthetist, a South African, who explained carefully the nature of my sedation. First, my forehead was to be injected with local anaesthetic in order that the stereotactic metal frame could be securely fitted onto my head. I would be sedated for this process, which was the drilling of the two holes in my skull which would receive the electrodes leading into my brain.

The sedation would be allowed to wear off somewhat as they finished the drilling and focused upon my physical reactions to the implants. This all seemed very straightforward, but it hardly mattered because by this stage there was no choice. I had to go through with it.

The anaesthetic room – like the one I had visited for my MRI – had a naïve astrological picture on the ceiling of children leaping happily over the stars. Soon the sedative started to work and I began to feel relaxed and no longer afraid of the intrusion into my skull. My surgeon was surrounded by a sea of faces all dressed in scrubs and smiling at me. my advanced practitioner nurse held my hand and another nurse held the other hand. I felt quite relaxed.

Then I was wheeled to the operating theatre and the job began. I put my trust in this surgeon who was about to meddle with my mind. I had already googled him and his credentials were impressive enough with a PhD from Cambridge, but my expectations were high. He looked a bit on the young side, but he had plenty of DBS experience.

The process of injecting my forehead was very uncomfortable, particularly the first one, but I reasoned dozily that complaining was pointless, the procedure would go ahead. I knew he would access my brain using a hand drill, like one at the hardware shop, and I could hear it loudly as it penetrated the bone.
It sounded more like a lesson in carpentry as he chatted to his assistant, but I was somewhat alarmed by his comment: "We seem to have a screw missing. Anyone seen it?" Lying flat on my back with the surgeon behind me it was impossible to know whether this was a joke or not. Either way, it could have some mileage as operation tales go.

I kept checking with the surgeon how far along we were. The last thing I remember him saying was "About three quarters of the way". Suddenly it was over and I was being wheeled to the CT scan room to check that everything was in order. I looked up and there was the clock 12:38: it had taken four hours.

Euphoria
I was euphoric because I had just succeeded. I had not succumbed to a brain haemorrhage; I was still alive and my limbs had reacted in the right way having been stimulated by the pacemaker during the surgical procedure. It was very encouraging. The operation had been a success, so far.
Back in the ward I had a look at myself and there were several big bruises on my forehead and a large sutured area on my scalp, but otherwise I looked remarkably normal. What was more remarkable was the fact that I could walk to the bathroom unaided even though I was quite shaky after the operation itself. Apparently, this was the "stun effect" which would not last (but it did last for three days). On the second day of my feeling normal first time in 14 years I was overcome with relief, amazement and humility.

After my daughter had alerted the world via social media to my forthcoming surgery emphasising the bravery and dangers involved. I felt I had to respond and I posted three messages. The first: "Thanks to being plugged into my pacemaker this morning for the first time in I can:
Type
Turnover in bed
Get out of bed in less than 10 minutes
WALK NORMALLY instead of shuffling
Go to the bathroom unaided
Use the WC instead of a commode
I have NO PAIN
A miracle!

This was approved by 49 friends. They also liked my later post: "After 14 years of screwing up my life, PD is going to have to SOD OFF."

Finally:
"I am sitting in the day room in the Neuroscience ward of the John Radcliffe Hospital reflecting on my good fortune. I have been treated by a team of world experts and cared for by an army of angels. The National Health Service (NHS) is a remarkable institution which we must preserve." My feelings were endorsed by many. I ended up in floods of tears. The doctor doing his rounds was somewhat taken aback, but I explained my love for the NHS and that these were tears of joy.

Recovery
Over the next few days I became familiar with the hospital routine.
06 00 – Blood pressure and temperature observations. This occurs every four hours and is heralded by a melodic three tone bleep. Bleeping from patients occurred throughout the night, often one

semi-tone apart in some kind of bizarre duet. 06 00 was a busy time for the night staff.

07 00 – Bed-making, general spruce-up of patients ready for the doctors' rounds.

08 00 – Breakfast. Although our room was positioned opposite the kitchen my hopes were dashed when the trolley apparently went to the whole round of the ward and ended up with us last. Nothing to get excited about though because NHS breakfast is pretty basic; just cereal.

09 00 – Doctors' rounds. You could tell when the doctors (almost all male) were coming because they are heralded by deep voices and the sound of expensive leather shoes creaking politely as they advance on the ward. There are accompanied by a flurry of nurses (almost all female) shuffling in rubber-soled shoes. Patients were addressed politely and without condescension in the case of elderly ones. I was pleased about this.

12 30 – Lunch. An excellent meal if you chose the Asian version. Otherwise somewhat stodgy.

15 00 – Visitors. A frenzy of emotion.

17 30 – Supper. A disappointment and likely to stick a while in the stomach.

20 00 – Night shift takes over, visitors leave.

22 00 – Attempt to sleep

04 00 – Give up sleep in favour of online Scrabble.

The next seven days I recovered from my first operation and prepared for the next. The stitches on the top of my head were annoying me somewhat and I wondered when I would be able to wash my hair. During these days, I was plugged into my pacemaker and my PD symptoms subsided. Most noticeable is the elimination of "off" periods to the extent that I began to forget when to take my medication because I did not get the normal reminder.

Several weeks earlier I had foolishly agreed to assist with some research projects while an in-patient in the Neuroscience block at the hospital. Little did I realise that this would involve going off my medication twice first thing in the morning and being scrutinised and graphed so that my various facets could be measured. The tests involved recalling number sequences and I was quite surprised by the results:
My highest score was 80% and my lowest was 70. Even Henry was very impressed. I was pleased that I didn't seem to have lost my memory as a result of DBS.

August 22 - Stage 2 surgery

The second operation was due to take place a week after the first on August 21st. I was prepared in the usual way. I started with a disinfectant shower using a "scrub", which made me smell like a public lavatory, but was guaranteed to kill 99% of MRSA bugs. The donning of the shapeless and back-opening hospital gown came next, followed by the fight with anti-DVT flight socks, the struggle to remove my wedding ring and the hours of waiting hungrily in bed for the porters to turn up. The meal trolley did its round many times I was unable to have anything. At first, they said I was second on the list and would be "done" that morning then somehow I slipped to third on the list and would be done in the afternoon. Then I slipped off the list entirely for that day. The one concession was that I was allowed to eat at 6 o'clock but I was to starve from 2 am next morning. Feeling a bit defiant and full of self-pity, I had a midnight feast at 01 55 when the nurses weren't watching and I scoffed the end of a box of chocolates.

The next morning was the same until 12 00 when I decided to complain, but just before I let rip, the men in blue turned up. It was time for me to "go down". I had two anaesthetists on the job and very soon they had a cannula in my hand and I was beginning to feel woozy as the initial sedative set in. I was to have a general anaesthetic this time. As I looked upwards, the kiddies in the astrological landscape on the ceiling started bobbing up and down crazily as I went under.

"Hello Briony, you've had your operation. It's time to wake up." I wonder why they always repeat this and very loudly. What I wanted at this stage is a bit of peace to be with Henry who was standing dutifully to my right. I was returned to the ward and the PD nurse explained what happened next and what to expect when I went home. I heard very little as I drifted in and out of sleep, but fortunately Henry was there taking notes. I remember looking at the clock at 3 20 and then the next time I looked it was 7 30 and I assumed it was the morning and breakfast time. When I learned that it was only evening and I had to get through a whole night, I was quite despondent. But it wasn't a problem and I just slept and slept the best part of 12 hours.

The pacemaker in my chest was no problem at first, though I was quite surprised by the length of the scar and stitch line. I noticed that they had shaved the under-side of my hair on the left side of my head so they could weave down under the skin connecting my brain electrodes to the pacemaker. That Saturday morning, I got ready to go home and the prospect was very exciting. I had been in hospital for 10 days and beginning to lose touch with the outside world. The car journey home was rather uncomfortable until I found the neck cushion to buffer the jerking from the brakes because my neck muscles were pretty sensitive.

It was a relief to be home and off my best behaviour. Things had changed in my absence: the beans and peas had grown and the two baby tortoises had hatched. Henry was going to work from home for the next two weeks while I recuperated.

August 23 – September 12: Early days back home

By the time I left hospital the benefits of several plug-ins had worn off and my old PD symptoms returned with some unwelcome new ones. I became immobile after 20 30 and had to go to bed. I was dribbling constantly night and day. Night times were a nightmare even when I took an extra 100g of Stalevo around 2 am. I still had great difficulty standing up and my only option was to use the commode.

I had expected the benefits I had experienced to wear off but I didn't expect to be dribbling and close to using a wheelchair. Added to this was the inflammation of my chest stitches which required another course of antibiotics from the local nurse. After five days of treatment and no improvement I started to worry that infection might force the removal of the pacemaker and the whole surgical procedure would have to be repeated. I rang the Advanced Practitioner Nurse at the hospital who told me to come in straight away

After she and the professor had inspected my stitches the verdict was that they were not infected after all, but I should keep an eye out for any adverse changes before having the stitches removed on Friday September 12.

6.5 Effects of the first DBS nine months post-operation.
Positive changes post DBS
No significant "off" times.
Reduction of drugs.
No dyskinesia
Reduced tremor
Better sleep
No diet restrictions

New side-effects of DBS
1. Freezing
Hesitance and imbalance occur when initiating walking and changing direction if I do not wait until fully functional. I have fallen eleven times since the operation in August 2014.

2. Breathlessness
When I bend over
When I walk
When I talk and walk
When I sing

3. Fatigue
I lack the stamina I had before the op.

4. Mouth problems
My tongue moves slowly which means that I must have small mouthfuls, must not talk with my mouth full and I take longer to clear my mouth. When I am eating my voice is very quiet. I dribble, which can be very embarrassing. My speech can often be slurred and quiet. Sometimes I am too exhausted to speak.

Symptoms which remain and have worsened from pre-operative times
Difficulty rising from a chair/getting out of bed at night.
Lack of dexterity - fumbling
Poor handwriting
Night sweats

Questions for the medics
Why do I always leave the hospital after a reprogramming and feel great, but about three weeks later the bad symptoms creep back?
Are the electrodes accurately targeting the STN?

Is it possible to correct the side-effects of DBS eventually?

6.6 DBS Post-operative assessment 2014-6

New symptoms require some adjustment and are very noticeable. It is very easy to forget those symptoms which have disappeared as a result the surgery and they are many. I decided to look at this objectively by giving weightings to symptoms depending on their seriousness and nuisance. (10 = very problematic, 1 = trivial). When estimating nuisance, the frequency, duration and intensity of the symptom is assessed. The + or - indicate whether the symptom is new (-) or has disappeared (+): See below:

New symptoms	Score
Drooling	-8
Gait freezing	-10
Weak voice	-8
Poor hand-writing/typing -	-7
Total loss	**-33**

Disappearance of old symptoms	
Off times	+9
Getting in /out of bed	+6
Sleeping	+6
Lack of tremor	+5
Lack of dyskinesia	+5
Total gain	**+31**

It would seem that the negative symptoms have marginally outweighed the positive ones. The net loss in this primitive cost/benefit analysis is 2. This is some kind of objective analysis but it's hardly scientific. I feel I have had to pay a price for this surgery. The surgical procedure went well and the early days were promising, but they did not last.

I have been called "brave" many times, which I deny. I don't consider myself brave because I elected to have this operation and the risks were relatively small. I have met some truly brave people in hospital who did not opt to be there like I did. They had been admitted to the neuroscience ward as an emergency, or had been living with the uncertainty of cancer. For many their admission was not planned, and the outcome of surgery was uncertain as was their future. But my case was entirely different: my diagnosis was correct, my surgery was planned and the good outcome was anticipated. I was one of the lucky ones on the neuroscience ward.

6.7 A second chance
DBS Surgery 2

I spent one week in hospital in February 2016 for general investigation and reprogramming. It appeared that they had more or less exhausted the system's possibilities. I was quite surprised when the team offered me the possibility of a second operation. This had been prompted by the introduction of new technology. Boston Scientific had produced new hardware and a programmer and I would be one of the first patients to be offered this chance. I agreed without hesitation: the current system offered me little in the way of therapy and on reflection the results one year on were mostly negative.

For the first time, 18 months after surgery, the reason for the poor response was revealed. One of my electrodes was off target, which could not be easily remedied without installing a completely new system. I wish they had told me sooner, although during stage 1 of that operation, I was aware that something had gone wrong with the second implant. I imagine that they had hoped to overcome this problem by careful post-operative programming – but it hadn't worked.

The proposed new surgery would involve removing all the hardware from the previous operation and installing the new equipment in a second operation four weeks later. This meant I would have to come into hospital to have the hardware removed and then wait four weeks without brain stimulation – a prospect I was not looking forward to. There were several cancellations during that time due to emergencies and my patience was running out.

The second stage when the electrodes were implanted, was by this time very familiar and I did not experience the same level of fear as in the previous operation. This time they hit the target (the STN) which took them 6 hours, but both electrodes were optimally placed. I knew the next four weeks (until the new system was activated) would be very difficult, especially at night. I became very dependent on Henry who had to lift me in and out of bed. Satin sheets and satin pyjamas were absolutely essential along with grab handles everywhere. Rigidity was the main problem I also experienced new ones such as dystonia, cramps and dyskinesia. It was sheer hell.

Four weeks later I returned the hospital to have the system switched on. The Boston system had several programmes and they were "directional". This meant that I had four programmes and a range of options within each. I knew it would take time to explore all the possibilities.

The recovery was swift and I was pleased with the results:

My balance was much better and the freezing had disappeared along with the falling.

Everyone commented on my improved speech; articulation and volume were much better.

My facial expressions were more animated and everyone said how "well" I looked. (I think they meant "fat"!)

There were several problems still:

Breathlessness was not improved; this was troublesome when I was out gardening, doing up my shoes and walking quickly especially uphill.

My left side was still weak and my left leg had to keep catching up with my right.

Dyskinesia during those first few months after the operation was persistent. It manifested itself in several ways – non-stop singing of 60s Motown hits, gibberish to the cats and absolute nonsense to the tortoises.

When on the bus, I had an irresistible desire to talk to everyone and help old ladies off the bus.

I am still trying to get a good balance between stimulation and medication. This is quite subtle and I have experienced quite alarming episodes of hyper-dyskinesia. For example, returning from the hospital overdosed on the bus.

Looking back over the last three years I have no regrets about having had the brain surgery. Admittedly, there are symptoms that I now I did not have prior to operations but perhaps this is just a sign of progression that I have to accept is ongoing, albeit slowly.

If I look around at people I have known with PD, their decline is obvious and I know that is where I would be if I hadn't had the surgery. I expect to have 5 -7 reasonable years and I can enjoy the grandchildren and some retirement. After that, any good years would just be a bonus. It is better to is not the set my expectations too high because I'll be disappointed.

REVIEW 6
When PD strikes it gives us no choice, but to grin and bear it. The timing is never ideal and its relentless progress continues to test us. At present, the treatment options are limited, but there are initiatives to investigate and choices to make. This gives patients a sense of power and control over their condition. Both clinical trials and DBS involve some degree of risk, but the encouraging outcomes make this worthwhile.

Key question
Why are potential DBS candidates so thoroughly screened?

Chapter 7
Facing the future

Introduction:
Facing the future is uncomfortable and burying our heads in the sand is the normal response. One thing is certain; PD will progress and currently there is no cure so we shall have to put up with it for the rest of our lives.

7.1 Objective measurements of PD
Standardised methods have been devised to quantify PD, monitor the response to treatment, assess quality of life and help to determine its progression.

The Unified PD Rating Scale (UPDRS)
This is a tool for objectively measuring the severity of the disease (see Glossary).

(Movement Disorder Society) PD Unified Rating Scale (MDS)
This scale has recently been revised and it is similar to the previous one which focused on severity of symptoms. This new one assesses the impact of symptoms upon the patient.

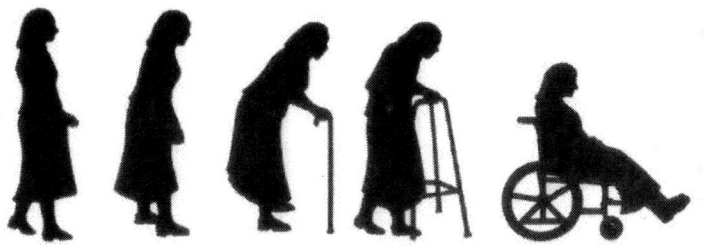

Fig. 9 Hoehn and Yahr Stages of Parkinson's.
Source: Jane Upton

The modified Hoehn and Yahr scale
(with two intermediate stages* included).

Stage 1	Symptoms on one side only.
Stage 1.5*	Symptoms on one side with some axial involvement.
Stage 2	Symptoms both sides without balance impairment.
Stage 2.5*	Symptoms both sides; very slight balance impairment on pull test (recovery from being pulled backwards).
Stage 3	Disease affects both sides with mild to moderate symptoms: some postural instability: physically independent.
Stage 4	Severe disability; still able to walk or stand unassisted.
Stage 5	Wheelchair – Confined to bed and wheelchair unless assisted.

Adapted from "Neurology pocket", A. Walker, Böhm Bruckmeier, 2012. Original publication by Hoehn and Yahr 1967.

7.2 Here's a timeline for how PD progressed for me:
1983 - First noticed tremor on left side during driving test.
1995 - Stiffness in back and neck developing.
1999 - Surgery to decompress stiff left shoulder.
2000 - PD diagnosis.
2001 - Started dopamine agonist (Cabergoline). Stopped due to nausea. Propranolol helped with anxiety at work.
2003 - Started Levodopa and continued to take Mirapexin.

2006 - Retired from teaching.
2007 - Set up local support group for young-onset PWP.
2007 - Fell asleep while driving and had to surrender licence.
2008 - Retired from International Baccalaureate examining.
2009 - Co-authored geography book.
2012 - Co-authored two more geography textbooks.
2013 - Moved out of house into a more Parkinson's-friendly one.
2013 - Joined local church choir.
2014 - Lifetime ambition fulfilled: I became a grandma to Sebastian.
2016 - Granddaughter Edith born.
2016 - Successful DBS surgery.
2016 - Began to write this book.

7.3 Timeline detail
2000-2006 Working with PD (0-6 years post-diagnosis)
I was in the wrong job, teaching geography. Clambering over rocks, wading through streams and digging pits were all part of the job. There were field trips too when we had to be in charge 24/7. But it was the everyday teaching that could cause a panic attack. Each time I walked towards the classroom the anxiety rose in my chest, my hands went clammy and another panic attack took over. It seemed as if PD was going to cramp my style and turn me into a nervous wreck. I had never suffered from lack of confidence, but PD sapped my self-assurance and I began to doubt my ability to take control of situations. Shaking in front of a class did not gain respect from them. And one comment from a student (not one of mine) made me finally give up after six years teaching with PD – "You see that teacher over there. Well, she's well weird". I was destroyed by that comment and even a reprimand by the head of his faculty would never put things right. I had to go.

2007–2011 The productive years (7-11 years post-diagnosis)

I retired in 2006 when I had qualified for a modest teacher's pension.

I did not lose touch with geography once I had settled into retirement. I wrote three textbooks for the International Baccalaureate course for which I was an examiner. I had a daily routine and generally I worked in the morning and gardened in the afternoon. I enjoyed being my own boss and remember one hot July afternoon realising that I was responsible to no-one and could please myself. So, I stood on the rockery and ate a choc-ice while singing the "Hallelujah" chorus to myself and my tortoises. Retirement was liberating, I discovered.

Once the anxiety of teaching was behind me I began to enjoy retirement. Seven to ten years post-diagnosis were some of the most productive, when I learnt about PD and became a patient advocate, joined societies, spoke publicly and ran a local young-onset PD support group.

It was during this period that I had my greatest independence. I was confident about travelling independently over long distances by train. I went to London to conferences run by The Cure Parkinson's Trust and I participated in conferences for Parkinson's UK. I worked on their interview panel and was on the editorial board for their quarterly magazine. I spoke on national BBC radio (the "You and Yours" programme, July 2010) about the national Sinemet (Levodopa) shortage, and on local radio with a consultant from King's College about non-motor symptoms. When it came to changing attitudes, my principal line of argument was that PD was a progressive and lethal disease despite attempts to play down its nastiness by some who wanted to soften the blow for the newly-diagnosed. We would get public support once they knew the truth: PD kills you but first it ruins your life for years.

A family trip to the USA to visit my brother David and his family marked the end of this creative and adventurous period. I knew that the scope for travel became more limited each year. David's family of five, now grown-up, children loved the big outdoors and took risks. We were to stay in their remote woodland holiday village – or rather a collection of woodland chalets, isolated and accessible only by boat. I would have my own chalet and would sleep alone.

I had a few moments of fear in the chalet knowing that there was no-one close by if I got in a predicament. I was keen to go fishing at 6 am in a small motorboat with my brother. I achieved all this, but kept it to myself. It was a private triumph to have taken these risks despite having PD.

2012-2014 Struggling (12-14 years post-diagnosis).
After the trip to the USA, my condition seemed to deteriorate. It wasn't that I developed new symptoms, but those that I already had intensified and became more frequent. The "on-off" syndrome was my primary difficulty. This meant that although I took drugs every three hours, they took a long time to kick in – sometimes up to an hour and a half – and then began to wear off before the three hours were up. The feeling of wearing off was heralded by a vice-like grip that took hold in my neck and spread down to my feet, gripping and contorting each muscle so that my whole body could not coordinate. My balance was thrown and I found it great take difficulty in manoeuvring from one position to another. My gait became a shuffle and turning on the spot was a major challenge.

But PD had its real triumph at night. Simply going to the bathroom was a major ordeal that required ingenuity. I acquired several aids which was symbolic of disability: a walking frame, a bed-handle, mattress raiser, a comfy chair and grab handles. I also devised some cunning ways of coping. My way was to get off the loo onto my knees and then it was easier to balance as I pulled up my pyjamas. Another way of freeing my hands was to prop myself against the wall. It became obvious that our house with its 46 stairs was no longer a suitable abode for us. I lost confidence in the night and felt terrified when trying to go down from the top landing: it was time to move. Which we did in 2013 and chose a 1960s two-storey house which is much more suitable for someone in my condition.

But motor problems were not my only ones. I also had gastro-oesophageal reflux. I visited the Enterology Department of the Royal Berkshire Hospital and no cause was found. This was principally because they had no appreciation of the profound effect of PD on my whole physical system. Each time I went to the hospital, I was in the "on" the state which meant that the only ever saw images of my oesophageal sphincter when it was functioning normally. I could not go to hospital independently without being well medicated, so they never saw reality and did nothing to remedy the problem even though I explained in writing the effect of PD on my gut.

Acid reflux made the absorption of drugs difficult, and increasingly I found it necessary to impose rigid time limits on taking pills and eating meals. All pills were to be taken 45 minutes before the meal and on an empty stomach. This becomes tricky when interval between pills is only three hours and they take one hour to kick in.

Travelling became very difficult because my "off" state was becoming ever more troublesome to deal with and often resulted in freezing and inability to walk. I could not cope with long-distance journeys by train. Also, I could never eat at the other end of a journey because I knew this could block the next set of pills. Drug-wise, I had tried everything: Mirapexin (prolonged release), Stalevo (the key source of Levodopa), Madopar dispersible (a good choice for getting you out of the predicament quickly), Madopar (prolonged relief to get you through the night). Incidentally, I wonder why PD drugs always come in childproof bottles. They are a nightmare to open when you have to cope with tremor and poor manual dexterity. The birth rate among pill-popping PWP must surely be low.

With reluctance, I gradually cut down my social activities. We seldom went out in the evening because I always went off by 9 30. I cut down my choir practices on Monday nights and was forced to give up my creative writing class because I did not have sufficient stamina to last two hours. I managed to continue singing in the village church choir because sessions were short and did not involve travelling. PD had deprived me of work and now it was to stifle my creativity. I was reaching the end of the road and knew that eventually it would crush my spirit.

7.4 Blog: The "Honeymoon Years" by Briony Cooke

Once upon a time someone without PD invented the expression "The honeymoon years". They were referring to the period between roughly 5 and 10 years post-diagnosis when we are supposed to have come to terms with and have learnt to live with this "unwelcome visitor"– PD.

Initially, I was puzzled by this expression. Life with PD was no honeymoon as far as I was concerned. It involved losses of freedom, independence, income and I had to cope with a punishing drug regime. I would certainly give the marriage a miss.

7.5 Blog: *Then and Now* by Briony Cooke
As an Easter present one year before my DBS operation, our children treated us all to a very welcome holiday in Cornwall. We stayed in a small coastal village where we had spent many happy family holidays 25 years earlier. Since then, our circumstances have changed: the three children have grown up, we have aged, I have retired, my husband has developed diabetes and I have got PD.

While sitting on a bench overlooking the sea, I noticed that the coastal features had not changed at all in those 25 years. There were the same caves, the same rocky wave-cut platform and the same stream meandering down the beach. But, of course 25 years is only a moment in geological time and social and economic changes occur much more rapidly and are more easily recognised. The village shop used to sell basic needs for self-caterers: tinned veg, bin-bags and faded copies of "Bunty" on the newsstand outside. But it is now a "Surf Shack" selling wetsuits to the surfing elite who were even visiting during this bitterly cold Easter holiday. Similarly, the farm shop which once sold limp lettuces and a tart or two is now stuffed with organic goodies and French delicacies like sun-dried tomatoes and tapenade to suit the well-heeled, well-travelled residents. The notice board indicates an affluent population with advertisements for hydrotherapy for dogs. If only People with PD could access this therapy too.

PD, which is a movement disorder, has had a significant effect upon my physical activity. Twenty-five years ago, I would have thought nothing of walking up the cliff path or picking my way over the rockpools. These days, I have to pick my moments and venture out well-medicated and not alone. Slopes and rough terrain are difficult because of balance problems. Stamina is much reduced by PD and walking is limited at times. The tables have turned and now I am the straggler.

There are many beach activities which I still enjoy: building sand-castles and diverting streams, all I need are some grandchildren. I used to enjoy surfing, not the athletic kind where you ride the waves skilfully balancing upright. My kind of surfing was done lying on a board and drifting ungracefully towards the beach. I know that I will never do this again mainly because the cold water, even in summer, would induce cramps and dystonia. Night times away from home are often problematic because I become immobile. On this holiday, I brought with me the essential equipment: satin pyjamas to turn over in bed, a rope ladder tied to the bed legs to pull me up and a leg hook to turn me round once sitting. The first night went badly because I couldn't reach the bedside light switch and dropped my pills all over the floor. However, compared to my night-times in 1988 with three noisy children and a three-year old who insisted on sharing our bed at 3am, these nights even with PD were a dream.

One of the most significant changes brought about by PD is upon my diet and meal routine. If I eat small, protein-free meals during the day and save my main meal until the evening, my medication works very well, but there is no spontaneity. It would have been nice to tuck into fish and chips or a pasty at lunch time and eat it on the quayside. Even more decadent would be to follow that with a scone and clotted cream – just a dream.

It would be very easy to blame PD for all these adverse changes over 25 years, but many result from ageing and it is very difficult to distinguish the two causes. These days I notice that friends of a similar age without PD complain about aches and pains and other symptoms which do not affect me at all.

Having PD does not exclude me from having a good time, but it does mean having to accommodate the condition by making changes and adaptations when away from home. Although there were some restrictions on the holiday, they did not in any way reduce the pleasure I got from staying in this stunning seaside environment and the company of my family.

7.6 Progression and prognosis

PD is a progressive illness, but the rate of progression is difficult to determine and varies between individuals. The symptoms may remain mild and unchanged for decades, but this is unusual and only 5-10% of cases experience little disability during the first 10 years. Alternatively, progression may be rapid in 5-10% of the PD population and the patient will become wheelchair-bound and totally dependent on others for their care and wellbeing. This is more usual when patients are diagnosed with "atypical Parkinson's". Examples are PSP (Progressive Supranuclear Palsy) and MSA (Multiple System Atrophy). Both these types are very rare.

7 REVIEW

This chapter deals with two difficult issues that some PWP are reluctant to confront: What stage is my PD now? How bad is it going to get?

I present two ways that doctors use to assess your condition objectively: the UPDRS and Hoehn and Yahr tests are objective and used to quantify your condition. By comparing test results over time, they can judge the rate of change in an individual.

Chapter 8
Minding the brain

Introduction:
Good mental health will also help you stay positive, though it's also a balancing act between knowing just enough to stay informed and not too much that it'll tip you over into anxiety.

8.1 Anxiety
Anxiety is a well-known feature of PD that may precede diagnosis, which in itself may generate more stress. Anxiety ranges from mild to severe. You may experience general restlessness associated with worry about how you will cope now and in the future. Anxiety in its extreme form can be quite disabling and might be described as a panic attack. In this latter case it is associated with intense fear, palpitations, breathlessness and nausea. The physical and psychological recovery from such an attack may take hours.

Sometimes the emergence of anxiety occurs when the situation that was previously responsible recurs: for example, a place where a fall occurred or a social gathering. Subconsciously recalling the event which caused such stress may stimulate a repeat performance. Worry about your ability to cope with a panic attack may deter the you from socialising. This may lead to isolation and further anxiety.

The changing relationship between knowledge and anxiety over time.

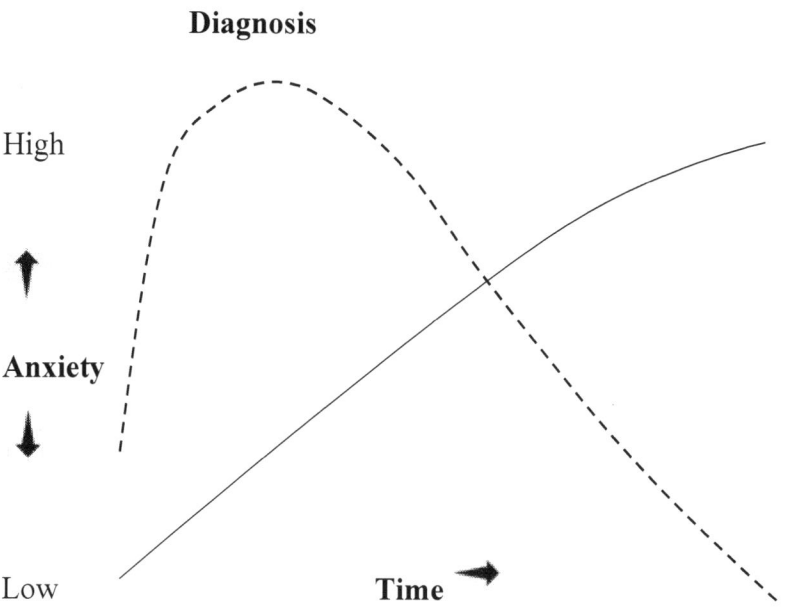

Fig 10 above, shows the response to diagnosis and the relationship between anxiety and knowledge.
Dotted line – Anxiety
Solid line - Knowledge

Initially, before diagnosis knowledge of PD is low. The diagnosis provides some knowledge of this condition, but most is acquired gradually over a number of years. Knowledge of the condition is gained by simply having it and also input by medics and your own research (assuming you have access to the Internet). But it is helpful to go beyond the basics and to ask questions when something problematic arises. Even at diagnosis there are many questions which either do not come to mind with the patient feels inhibited about asking.

This anxiety curve shows a dramatic increase immediately before diagnosis associated with the uncertainty of what lies ahead then the level gradually declines with time and the gradual increase in knowledge. The assumption is made that knowledge is good and the anxiety is detrimental. This may be true in most cases, but sometimes too much knowledge can generate anxiety. Some PWP will reach saturation point which may result in burying their head in the sand. This type of escape from reality may be a form of self-protection and is to be commended if it alleviates stress.

8.2 Blog: *Panic by Briony Cooke*

As a teacher, I experienced more than one panic attack which was demoralising and stressful. I remember the racing heartbeat, the sweating and the extreme fear. I had to escape quickly to the staffroom where I could seek refuge. It is acutely embarrassing as a teacher to lose control in this way. I can look back now and the solution seems so easy. I should have relaxed and discussed the issue with students; I just did not have the strength to do that at the time.

When I was first diagnosed I would walk down the busy high street of the large town where we lived convinced that every time a stranger's gaze fell on me they were thinking I looked weird or in some way abnormal. Self-consciousness was a major feature of anxiety.

Eventually, I discovered how to cope with the problem of anxiety which dominated those first few years. CBT (cognitive behavioural therapy) helped me to understand the thought processes driving my behaviour. I had six sessions with a psychiatrist which seemed to remove the fear. There were other factors that may have simultaneously played a part.

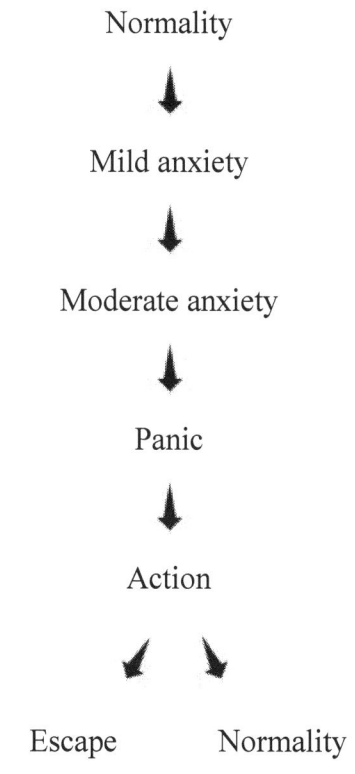

Fig. 11 The anxiety progression at the supermarket check-out.

The anxiety progression shows the effect of a situation that induces stress. The situation is normal at first, but as the exposure to stress increases the symptoms of anxiety magnify until the person decides to escape

Anxiety often starts when a situation is revisited where a previous panic attack occurred.

For me, the supermarket check-out was such a place. The bigger the shop, the greater the panic.

Recall of a previous attack raises alarm and induces symptoms. Further anxiety occurs as I worry that people in the queue will see my tremor.

They may realise that it may be part of a disease and therefore not my fault, or they may consider me a bit of a weirdo because the check-out freaks me out. I feel dominated by my symptoms and out of control.

The symptoms I experience are anxiety, sweating, palpitations and shallow breathing which are impossible to suppress and are self-sustaining.

The final decision is to flee or to stick it out and hopefully to recover.

Coping strategies:

It was about two years after diagnosis that my tremor increased and I became very self-conscious. I was not yet taking Levodopa and could not suppress the panic once it set in.

It was my youngest son, Chris (then in his early 20s) who worked in the supermarket at the time and had already lived with type 1 diabetes since the age of five. He would always tell me the truth and at the same time make realistic suggestions. His advice was Invaluable:

Start checking out with just one item then gradually increase the number.

He said that I should try to convince myself that the check-out operators do not care and do not notice your symptoms. The same goes for the people in the queue.

Make sure that you avoid fumbling by having your change ready.
Tell them that you need time because you have PD.
This final strategy is by far the most successful, but you may not yet feel comfortable about telling people.

8.3 Depression in PD
Why does depression occur in PD?
There are two arguments concerning the origins of depression with PD. First is the biological one, which claims that PD depression is a direct result of biological changes in brain and many of the brain chemicals affected by the illness are also implicated in the mood changes with depression. Secondly, the psychological one is that in PD it is a reaction to the disabling nature of the disorder; the loss of important roles, restriction of activities and increased dependence on others.

Given its frequency of occurrence and debilitating effects, many newly diagnosed patients are anxious about the prospect of depression. Very often they will try to find out the level of risk in their case. A previous history of depression seems to greatly increase the chance of the individual becoming depressed at some stage during the course of PD progression. The individual may have some biological predisposition to depression, or he/she may be the type of person who reacts to any stressful event by becoming depressed.

The age group most likely to succumb to depression would be termed as "young onset". Between the ages of 40 and 60 people are likely to still be working, and have dependent children. Parents in this age range may find themselves with spare money and time to enjoy themselves for the first time in many years. PD may directly challenge this freedom and the threat of losing it may be difficult for some people to bear.

In contrast, when PD starts later in life, particularly after normal retirement age, the individual may feel that his or her chances of living a full life have been more or less fulfilled. Furthermore, as noted earlier, many of the necessary adjustments to retirement may already have been made. Older people probably have low financial commitments or have already learned to reduce their outgoings. This is not to say that older people do not suffer from a diagnosis of PD, but its impact is greatest with those aged under 50.

8.4 Communication breakdown

Communication is a lifeline, a two-way interaction requiring effort and acceptance on both sides. The PWP is battling not only with the symptoms and frustrations of the disease, but also with the attitudes and responses of other people (Refer to Chapter 2 on diagnosis). Communication is a social skill and the way we communicate determines how we are perceived by other people. Sometimes because of communication difficulties, PWP are considered by others to have undergone a personality change. Consequently, they may be treated differently and possibly with less respect.

Body language, gesture, facial expression and posture all reinforce the content and meaning of what we are saying. We use movements, smiles, frowns etc, but all body language is affected by PD. Facial expression is diminished and misunderstanding is a consequence of this. The PWP might be considered to be bored or not interested.

The social interaction between people one of whom has PD may be limited by lack of eye contact and freezing of those muscles concerned with speech. This means the PWP may not react in time and there is a delay in initiating discussion and also in continuing it. Nuances in a conversation such as indicate pleasure or anger may also be lost.

Respiration is one of the most important functions of speech system. Over 80% of PWP have decreased lung function and shallow breathing. The voice may be coarse, strained and tremulous and the low volume makes two-way interaction difficult.

Poor articulation, slurring (dysarthria) combined with lack of breath control many give the impression that the PWP might be drunk; this misinterpretation is compounded by the instability of their gait.

Cognitive impairment is common in PD and can be severe hindrance to speech. The main problem is word finding and the delay caused by this may give the impression that the person is not interested in the topic. The inability to respond quickly causes breakdown in conversation.

These problems can be remedied to some extent if addressed by a speech and language therapist. Contact one as soon as you begin to show some of these symptoms.

The problems of communication may also be connected with poor hearing. Typically, PWP do not have hearing problems, but they may be blamed for having a relatively quiet voice which the partner cannot hear. This can be resolved very easy by the use of hearing aids. Unfortunately, in this situation where the PWP is constantly misheard and misunderstood, they may give up on conversation, because the effort required is just too much.

Problems of communication mentioned above can be addressed in a number of ways by those who care for the PWP.

You should:
Maintain eye contact
Listen and do not interrupt
Allow the patient plenty of time to respond
Do not finish a sentence for them
Do not pretend that you understand when you don't
Do not interrupt
Always face the person when speaking and listening

The breakdown of communication is serious problem with PD. It can isolate the patient and cut them off from all social interaction. Lack of communication can lead to loss of self-esteem and serious depression. It should not be underestimated. In the advanced stages of PD when the patient may be confined to a wheelchair is even more important that their contributions to conversations are noticed and a response is given. In general, the public is unaware of this problem which leads to serious frustration for the PWP.

Hypomimia

Hypomimia is masking of facial expression and is typical of advanced PD. It is due to paralysis or weakening of the facial muscles. It gives the impression that the patient is uninterested or cross; this leads to lack of response and introversion by the patient.

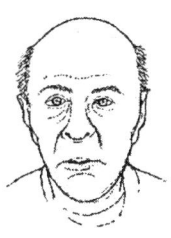 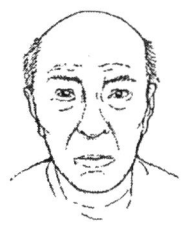 

Fig. 12
Left - The patient's expression is vacant.
Centre - The eyes are staring and they appear aggressive.
Right - The asymmetrical expression results from relative muscle weakness on the patient's left side.

8.5 Invisibility

This starts with people watching the tremor in your hands and ignoring the words from your mouth. Having PD is much more than a tremor: the disease is widely known, but the severity of the condition is at best underestimated.

Invisibility is almost inevitable because, as the disease advances, our ability to communicate effectively diminishes:

Our voices become quieter and our articulation begins to fail.

Our faces lose expression and we are perceived as angry or uninterested.

Our reactions are slower so we cannot join in discussion easily.

We prepare ourselves for an event that takes place outside the home by timing our medication carefully so that we are at peak performance. But we know that this is unreliable and so often it goes wrong. This discourages us to the point we may no longer go out. We end up silenced and imprisoned in our homes.

We are not always to blame; it's important to realise that the problem of invisibility partly depends upon people's ability to receive us.

The political consequences of invisibility

The invisibility that PD creates for individuals has profound political consequences. People are less aware of the severity of the disease, and therefore the funding is a relatively low priority for governments. People with advanced PD cannot speak for themselves, whereas those with other conditions such as heart disease, multiple sclerosis, cancer, AIDS/HIV can still communicate and their charities are likely to attract much more funding.

The actor Michael J. Fox wrote about his seven-year struggle with PD before he "came out". Fox stated:
"I had hidden my symptoms and struggles very well: through increasing amounts of medication, through surgery, and by applying hundreds of little tricks and techniques the PWP learns to mask his or her condition for as long as possible. While the changes in my life were profound and progressive I kept them to myself for a number of reasons: fear and denial to be sure, but I felt it was important to me just quietly to soldier on."

Trying to hide our symptoms may not be in our best interest. If we struggle at the checkout or bank, a quick "Sorry, I have PD; and I am slow and fumble a lot." This will bring understanding and a further few words such as "Still, I can't complain, at least I can still walk" will get the following messages across:

PD is a nasty and progressive disease.
It does not affect only older people.

8.6 Dementia

PD will affect a person's movements, but it can also impact their thought processes, mental function and memory. The result can be a condition called PD dementia.
This condition is caused by deposits in the brain of compounds called alpha-synuclein. These protein deposits are called Lewy bodies.

Symptoms associated with this dementia are:

- anxiety and irritability
- delusions
- depression
- difficulty in sleeping well at night
- difficulty in speaking clearly
- difficulty taking in what is seen and interpreting it
- memory changes
- paranoia
- visual hallucinations

Doctors can have difficulty diagnosing dementia because there isn't one test can definitively say a person has dementia or a specific dementia type. However, an MRI scan will reveal any changes that could be linked to dementia.
There is no known cure for PD dementia. Treatments include antidepressants such as serotonin; Clonazepam improves sleep. Dementia with PD tends to reduce life expectancy.

8 REVIEW

The psychological aspects of PD are more difficult to identify and control than the physical aspects. During the course of this disease many will have to live with problems such as dementia which presents their family / caregivers with may practical difficulties.

Key question.
Distinguish between anxiety and depression and identify the main symptoms of each.

Chapter 9
Issues and practicalities

Introduction:
With time PD becomes increasingly difficult to manage. Uncomfortable decisions have to be made over when to retire or to stop driving. For many PWP these decisions involve surrender and can cause a sense of loss.
Once retired, you might discover your loss of domestic capabilities and simple tasks become a chore. Cooking a meal, mowing the grass, or answering the phone can be testing and multi-tasking can be impossible.

9.1 Domestic deskilling
The deskilling process imposed by PD leaves you domestically less effective. You experience balance problems, tremor, slowness of movement, muscle weakness and reduced ability to smell. These make domestic tasks difficult to carry out and food preparation quite hazardous. If you were the principal cook or gardener before PD was diagnosed, the chances are that it will stay that way.
Domestic set-ups can vary significantly, but the family or friend(s) with whom you live will most likely assume that you will continue in these roles because they may not be aware of your limitations.
Christmas is a time of great domestic pressure and the Blog – Yuletide Challenge - discusses all the catering and domestic planning involved. After several years post diagnosis, you may need to take a step back and let others take over. This would be far more desirable than being completely exhausted by Christmas.

9.2 Blog: Yuletide Challenge by Briony Cooke. December 2013
Having moved house only three months ago, the sensible thing to do would be to have a quiet Christmas enjoying the solitude of this peaceful village. Instead, we are having a frenzy of guests for a period of 10 days, peaking at 14 on Christmas Day. They are coming from far and wide and some staying overnight. This prospect would intimidate many, but I am not going to let my PD get in the way of having a good time. The recipe for survival and enjoyment involves careful forward planning and delegation of duties.

I no longer drive which is a problem at Christmas when we feel the need to overload ourselves with food to last the entire winter. Henry (husband) is only free to drive at weekends and has to work around Christmas. This means getting in, by car, the basic and bulky items which often run out, then perishables closer to Christmas by bus or train. I have limited the turkey to 5kg in weight, which should easily fit into the cat's designer pushchair along with the bacon and sausages. Without this remarkable vehicle designed for fat cats or small dogs, food shopping would be difficult. When I get it home, I shall have to store the turkey in the cold garden shed with the three hibernating tortoises.

Once the big day comes and all the guests are here, my role will be bossing, not cooking. Fortunately, we have several very good cooks in the family who will take over the difficult tasks of lifting and pouring, and hopefully avoid the kind of mess that I leave behind every time I cook: flour scattered, lard splattered and a trail of drips to the waste bin. Cooking with Parkinson's is always messy and often hazardous. It impairs my balance, and lifting a heavy turkey out of the oven is impossible. Slow-motion mashing and whisking are impractical with hungry guests waiting. Also, my sense of smell is poor, which results in frequent burnt offerings and, at worst, a fire risk.

We have several dietary complications: my Parkinson's imposes a rule of no protein in the day time; the three diabetics should have meals on time and reduced sugar; two others need reduced fat and carbohydrate respectively, and then there's the cat's Addison's disease and yet more pills to remember. The timing of Christmas Dinner is crucial, and 6 pm is the best slot. However, I shall have to delay mine until 9 pm to ensure that my evening dose of Levodopa is effective and I can join in the festive fun without having to go to bed early.

The sleeping arrangements are complicated given the numbers involved and the age range from 0–89. There will be no room here to accommodate the expectant couple, who will stay at the inn up the road... possibly in their stable! Our other guests will stay here, although the in-laws will have to share their bedroom with 3 baby tortoises. They are not much trouble provided I remove them to our bedroom at night or maybe the airing cupboard (i.e. the tortoises).

Already, I have allocated tasks. Several meals will be cooked by one of our sons, the other will be the taxi driver, and our daughter will provide some accommodation. I am going to take it easy and will not appear in the morning until my medication is working and I am functional; breakfast will be "do-it-yourself". I shall take a nap after lunch to make up for my interrupted night-time sleep and I shall take a healthy walk along the river each day.

I shall also behave badly. I shall eat as much chocolate as I fancy and repent at my leisure in the New Year.

9.3 Work and early retirement

The following are four accounts of individual experiences. The particular challenges varied with the type of employment, but there are some common observations.

Telling employers was not always a priority

Colleagues were generally understanding and responded appropriately

Job security was important

Adjustments to work practices and commitments were made

Six months' enforced sick leave was stressful

Stress is much relieved by retirement.

9.4 PWP Experiences
Blog: Challenges faced by employees with Parkinson's, by Nigel Crabb.
I am married with two grown-up sons and was diagnosed with early-onset Parkinson's in May 2006, aged 44. Like many younger people who finally get diagnosed with Parkinson's, the road to that conclusion was long and I can trace my symptoms back at least four years before that.

As someone with Parkinson's in full time employment, I can share my experience of fulfilling the requirements of a busy job while managing both the symptoms of the disease and the side-effects of the essential medication. Of course, not everyone's job is the same. Mine, for example, has no significant physical demands other than those associated with commuting and other business travel. I spend much of my time in front of a computer and on the telephone which can be both a blessing and a curse. I am frequently required to present to both small and large groups of people (including customers) and, managing a large international team, lead many face-to-face meetings every week.

Everyone working with Parkinson's must make their own decision when it is the right time to tell their employer and colleagues about their condition. This will depend on many factors such as the type of job they do, the degree to which Parkinson's is impacting their performance (and safety) at work and whether they would benefit from the company making adjustments to their work or working environment. So far, I have chosen to tell very few people. I suppose my biggest concern with making my Parkinson's general knowledge is the fear of being treated differently (especially by those who work for me) and of people incorrectly associating something I do or say to Parkinson's. As far as I am concerned, as long as my performance and safety is not adversely affected and I can comfortably cope with the demands of the job, there is no need to draw attention to Parkinson's – it simply doesn't deserve to be the star of the show!

One of the commonly associated symptoms of Parkinson's is tremor but it is important to note that everyone's Parkinson's is unique and the amount of tremor can vary considerably. Hand tremor especially on my left side is my nemesis. Tremor is greatly influenced by factors such as excitement, stress, tiredness and whether the medication is working effectively (it doesn't always). It's hard to control a tremor and quite exhausting if you have to focus on doing so over a long period. For me tremor is one of the most embarrassing symptoms as it's hard to hide.

In my job, communication in written and verbal form is part of everything I do. Unfortunately, Parkinson's is very good at interfering with that. In fact it's as if Parkinson's is on a mission to inhibit one's ability to communicate before it gets going seriously on stopping you moving! I have taken a course of speech therapy to help reverse a decrease in the volume of my voice (common in Parkinson's patients as we think we are speaking louder than we really are) and to improve diction. It grows frustrating when you are constantly being asked to repeat what you have said or to speak up! Then, because of reduced dexterity in my hands and fingers, I have found writing and typing to be increasingly problematic. My writing is often small and illegible, even to me. Typing has become tiresome as I keep hitting the wrong key, missing keys or double hitting. Some people have problems using a conventional mouse for similar reasons. There are devices available, such as keyboard guards, to assist with these problems. Voice recognition software can also make a big difference.

We also communicate through our body language and especially through our facial expression. Once again Parkinson's likes to play tricks with that. People with Parkinson's are often described as wearing a 'mask' or having a vacant stare. In my case I know people sometimes read my feelings or mood incorrectly and I can come across as insincere when what I say isn't supported by what my face is saying. I'm sure this must be very confusing for others! I have to be aware of this all the time and remember to consciously "inform my face" of how I am feeling!

I mentioned above that sitting in front of a computer for long periods is both a blessing and a curse. It a blessing that the physical demands of my job are low (I know someone with Parkinson's who was a scaffolder – imagine that!). The curse is that, unless, I remember to regularly get up, stretch and walk around I will find myself in a lot of trouble with pain and stiffness. All Parkinson's patients know they must "use it or lose it" when it comes to keeping mobile which is why I maintain a regime of going to the gym and walking. Long meetings (where I am only participating) are a problem for the same reason. I will always sit near the door if I can otherwise I can be afflicted with minor anxiety attacks. I have to be able to get up and get out of the room when I feel I need to.

Business travel can be exhausting for people without Parkinson's but for me, flying three or four times a month together with the hotels, taxis and inevitable late nights would now be intolerable. I am able to split my working week between home and office which reduces the stress of driving (into London in my case). I am very conscious of not driving when I am too tired so tend to avoid the evening rush hour by leaving the office early and finishing my emails and phone calls from home. My position and job affords me the luxury of making these choices without seeking permission but most people would rely on their employer making these very necessary adjustments either proactively or on request.

This leads into the subject of how an employer responds when an employee with Parkinson's chooses to share the diagnosis and seek help. Parkinson's in working age people is not common so employers are likely to be less than knowledgeable about the disease or have a very distorted view of Parkinson's based on experience with much older people – relatives perhaps. As I mentioned above, Parkinson's is a very personal experience affecting everyone in different ways with different symptoms emerging at different times and with varying ferocity. Therefore there is no "one size fits all" when it comes to making adjustments for the employee. The employee and their neurologist are the experts – not the employer, not the company doctor and not even the employee's GP in most cases. The employer should listen to what the employee needs at any particular time as the disease progresses and, hopefully, feel able to make reasonable adjustments to allow the employee to continue to be as effective

as possible. All employees want to contribute and make a difference when they come to work and there is no reason why Parkinson's should prevent that!
In summary, being at work is good for me. Keeping busy and maintaining a positive outlook is absolutely essential to my wellbeing. I know I will need to turn to my company for help at some point and a caring and understanding employer, like I'm sure mine is, will make all the difference in the world. People with Parkinson's should be able to work as long as they feel able to – in fact they should be positively encouraged to work. Staying active, engaged and interested in the wider world is the best way to fight back.

Update
This document was originally written in 2011 and updated in 2014. What follows brings this document up-to-date as of July 2017.

With the support of my manager and GP, I formally went onto a long-term sickness programme in 2015 as I was not performing at the level I expected of myself. Interestingly, my managers said they had not noticed any decline in performance. I managed a large multi-national team and, for me, an underperforming leader was just not acceptable. I had already made reasonable adjustments in my work schedule and work location including a four-day week and working mostly at home. Neither of these really helped as the job I was doing still had to get done.

Everyday stress was making me feel very unwell. In the afternoons I felt so tired that I was unable to stay awake.
By the time I started on sick leave, I was being far more open about having Parkinson's both at work and outside work. This was a good decision and my fears of being treated differently

were largely unfounded. It was also no longer necessary to expend energy trying to hide the symptoms.

I am in regular contact with my UK manager and we even meet for lunch on occasions. We are currently exploring the possibility of me taking on a one- or two-day a week role which I can do from home as an individual contributor rather than a manager. I'm finding that having structure to my week (I've recently added regular swimming to my exercise regime) keeps me busy. If this new part-time role works out then I can see it providing cognitive stimulus alongside my important physical routine.

Despite the relentless progression of my Parkinson's, my symptoms started to improve when I stopped working. I was also able to stop taking one of my medications which had particularly nasty side effects. Tremor is far less bothersome now I am out of such a stressful environment. But Parkinson's is unforgiving and am now far more prone to freezing, loss of balance and falling. A bad fall in April 2016 required surgery to my hand and two nights in hospital.

Finally, it remains important to stay positive and optimistic even with the occasional setbacks.

Blog: Taking ill-health retirement, by Margaret Deacon
When I was diagnosed my husband John and I were both working. I was in an educational managerial role and John was in the printing industry. We had two daughters aged 23 and 27 who were both working at the time and our eldest daughter had presented us with a granddaughter.

We had recently celebrated our silver wedding anniversary and 50th birthdays and we felt hopeful about the future. We were determined to have a good time, to enjoy our grandchildren, and *to travel. The future seemed rosy – until I got my PD diagnosis in 2007. The consultant told us that it was important we did all our long-distance travel now because the future with PD was uncertain. We had been keen to visit relatives in Canada. However, we soon realised that PD might prevent us from fulfilling this dream. At the time my earnings were the main source of income and I couldn't say how long I would be able to work. John had been made redundant and the future did look grim.*

As a family, we had very little idea of what to expect with PD even though my grandmother had suffered with it. Our daughters encouraged me to find things out about PD but I was so wrapped up in my work; I became paranoid about getting everything done. Maintaining standards was important.

I had my suspicions about PD before I went to the consultant. Prior to the appointment I told the female members of my team at work about my suspicions and to make me feel at ease they joked about it. After my appointment with the consultant, I rang my secretary to give her the diagnosis. The general response from my colleagues was very supportive particularly from the women but the men found it more difficult to discuss. I took early retirement four years later.

My diagnosis was just the beginning of our troubles: my husband was diagnosed with diabetes two years afterwards. There were several members of his family who had diabetes so this was nothing new. I was not worried about this provided that he followed the regime and took the tablets. Eventually, after losing weight, he went to the doctor: he was in deep trouble. He was diagnosed with pancreatic cancer, but to soften the blow, the doctor said it was the best type of cancer to get as its progression was slower than most other types. He hated being in hospital and refused to stay. Those weeks were extremely difficult because I couldn't cope with the stress of his being at home. Eventually, he had his wish and came home to die.

I have managed two-and-a-half years alone and I'm pretty active with the daily tasks of living and looking after my elderly mother whom I visit most days, but I do get lonely. I am particularly so when putting down the phone after a long conversation with a family member or friend. I am concerned about my future. When I was diagnosed, my daughters told me not to worry, they would sort it out, but it's now ten years on and I need to raise the issue again.

Blog: Working with PD by Howard Jarvis
I was working as Clerk of Works for University of Reading when I was diagnosed with PD in 2010. But things had been missed or ignored years earlier, as it paled into insignificance as the pressures of managing an engineering consultancy during the construction market crash of 2008 and nursing my wife who had a catastrophic brain haemorrhage in May 2009 became more demanding.

The realisation and diagnosis of PD came gradually, the first significant incident was catching my left heel on the floor whilst walking – a problem I had put down to a badly broken ankle from 1996 which had set badly following complications. The orthopaedic surgeons at the Nuffield Hospital in Oxford suggested straightening the limb with an Illizaov fixator in 2005, and desperate to get back to playing sports, I went for it. After five months in a frame and the physiotherapist following, my left heel was still catching as it swung through. The PD symptoms worsened over time until I was stumbling round on major construction sites, losing grip in my left hand and getting coats on and off became a struggle.

I eventually went to the GP who referred me to neurology. Still oblivious to PD and thinking I'd trapped a nerve, I attended the Royal Berkshire Hospital and saw one of the consultants. I had been in the room about five minutes when he said "I've observed that your left arm doesn't swing and your blink rate is slow, these symptoms together with the notes suggest that you have Parkinson's. You will need a CT scan to make sure it is nothing more serious. I'll write to your GP and recommended some drugs. Good morning Mr. Jarvis." That was it: I left there stunned and speechless!

I quit my consultancy practice to care for my wife in 2009 and took six months' unpaid leave, then took the job as Clerk of Works at the University. It was half a mile away so I could get home quickly if needed. The PD diagnosis came in March 2010, but by 2012 symptoms were getting to the point where it was unsafe for me to do construction site inspections on rough ground, climb ladders and scaffolding. I had to confess that I had PD and was no longer safe on site. The works doctor agreed and, because there was no other work in my specialist field, I had to retire on ill-health grounds in February 2013. I was fortunate to have always paid my pension contributions right from apprenticeship to retirement.

Blog: Early retirement - by a former airline pilot (anonymous)
Immediately after my PD diagnosis I spoke to the British Airline Pilots' Association doctor. He explained that there were several pilots flying with a Parkinson's diagnosis, he went on to describe the procedure I would have to go through.
Firstly, I had to notify the airline then I was immediately put on sick leave as my flying licence was suspended and the CAA (Civil Aviation Authority) was informed. I had to wait about six weeks before I was able to see a CAA neurologist, a very kind and understanding man. He declared that I was fit to fly, but with a

stipulation on my licence of 'As or with', which meant as a co-pilot or with a co-pilot. I would then see the CAA neurologist every six months.

The airline encouraged me to apply for a Command which meant training to become a Captain, as it was obvious my career would be cut short and this would enhance my pension. I managed to fly for four years before I needed to take Levodopa which meant I would no longer be able to fly.
I applied for any Command vacancies that there were and at the time got my 13th choice which was on the Tristar out of Gatwick. I then had to complete a very intensive Command course on that aeroplane. After the ground school there was a period in a simulator where all sorts of system failures are thrown at you for you to cope with, and as a Captain you have overall command.

Some people have what is termed 'a gross event' where there is a great deal of fumes in the cockpit which can cause immediate symptoms of damage, nausea leading on to other complaints. I never had 'a gross event', but frequently flew the Boeing 757 first thing in the morning when there would regularly be a waft of an oily smell which only lasted a few seconds. I was tested at University College London by and was found to have PCBs in my blood.

9.5 Journeys with PD
Travel is a challenge when you have PD, but with plenty of preparation you can enjoy it and the experience is liberating. Long haul travel especially when you're crossing time and climatic zones requires a fair amount of planning. The advice given below would apply to all sorts of transport, but particularly to air travel.

Assistance
Always use this at airports and stations because it will be hugely helpful when trying to check-in and board the plane. If you have any doubts about what you can take on board, please ask the airline staff well in advance.

Medication
Remember to take enough medication to last you beyond the length of your stay away from home. For example, if you are staying away for one week, take two weeks' medication. Also remember to split packets between your luggage in case one piece gets lost. You should also take the prescription for your current medication. You may also need to take non-PD medication for things like headaches and tummy trouble.
Medical Insurance – Pre-existing conditions such as PD may make this more expensive.

ID
This is particularly important if you have a pacemaker of any kind. The DBS neurostimulator embedded in your chest is an example of this, and you must be very careful to bring with you a written statement from your hospital and a pendant with your identity. In the unfortunate event of your having to be hospitalised, this medical information will be essential for any medical procedure which could take place. If you take the handbooks with your DBS remote control you will be able to read about the risks.

Security
Currently, security is very tight. People with DBS systems will probably be advised by their hospital to avoid going through the security arch at the terminus. If you're in any doubt about this, show them the ID letter from the hospital. They are usually happy to give you a hand search instead of sending you through

the arch, but you will have to explain the situation to them. The term "pacemaker" is usually understood, but not "neurostimulator". Some security systems are "pacemaker safe".

Food and drink
If you have particularly difficult eating times which do not conform to the normal route, discuss this with your flight attendant. Always have a bottle of mineral water with you.

Sleep
Get plenty of sleep before you leave home and take a neck cushion for the journey. Unfortunately, you will need to plan your trips to the WC. There is little more demoralising than wobbling about in public when you are "off". Talk to your doctor about the possibility of taking medication at night which will help you through this kind of embarrassment.

Blog: Beating the queues, by John Inglis
While snaking my way to the US customs in Miami, I found myself brought to the front of a new queue by loud Hispanic lady with lots of large badges and a belt with a number of unfamiliar attachments, who turned out to be a 'US CUSTOMS' person who told you which queue to go in. My wife had played the Parky card I was allowed to skip the queue.

The only other time was when we were on our way to Atlanta airport where we had a 45-minute slot to change onto a plane going to our final destination. My wife was concerned that our time to be called to board was after a whole raft of different categories, e.g. first class, families with children, those with difficulty walking, airline loyalty club members, partner airline members, etc, and we fell into the last category. What this meant was that there would be no overhead storage for our cabin bags which would then be taken and stored in the hold which meant there would be the inevitable delay at the destination while they got our bags out of the hold, and we had the ongoing flight. Again, my wife played the Parky card and we boarded almost immediately and took our seat and luggage space ahead of all the rest. I had to slow her down as we went down to walkway to the plane and remind her that since I was being a Parky, we should walk slowly and at least look as if we had some level of difficulty walking. Needless to say we got our next flight on time!

Blog: The benefits of a cruise for those with PD by Karen Green
One of the main things that I enjoy about cruising is having a constant base: your well fitted out cabin. The feeling of security begins when your luggage arrives outside your cabin door having last been seen at the airport check-in.

The key feature of a cruise which continues to attract me is the variety of interesting destinations. We sail overnight arriving at a new destination usually between 7am and 9am. This can usually be a picturesque arrival but occasionally a rusty commercial dock.

We are never bored. There's on-board entertainment every night of varying types and quality. There are also daytime activities and talks.

The standard of food usually of a good and sometimes excellent. There is the option to dine alone if you wish at the same group table each night and the alternative option of turning up unbooked and arranging to share a table with others who have done the same. We find that we meet a lot of interesting people that way and I can go at a time that suits me on that day depending on my pill schedule and whether I am "on" or "off". Breakfast is very busy and I opt for breakfast in my cabin.

The sun decks are very busy on sea days as is the lunchtime buffet.

The balcony is great for sitting on in the early morning when you can't sleep.

Trips from the ship allow for a wide range of abilities and disabilities as do activities on-board.

There is provision for mobility scooters and plenty of lifts provide accessibility to those with mobility problems.

Blog: On the Buses by Briony Cooke
I have been a regular bus user since giving up driving ten years ago when I fell asleep at the wheel of my car and ended up in a hedge. Daytime somnolence and night-time insomnia are symptoms of PD and incompatible with safe driving. Having surrendered my licence, I received the compensation of a free bus pass. Living at that time near the centre of a large town, I could take full advantage of its efficient bus network. A bus pass is one of the few perks of having PD.

Getting geared up for a bus ride requires some forward planning. The first rule is to locate the bus pass and place in an accessible pocket. This avoids fumbling and tremor when getting on the bus with a long queue of grizzling toddlers waiting behind. Fashion is second to practicality and in winter an anorak and small rucksack are essential. Negotiating the central aisle with the bus in motion requires free hands to grab the rails and avoid embarrassing close encounters with complete strangers. Other challenges include floor hazards such as over-sized shopping bags, projecting feet and small dogs.

Once I have found a downstairs seat, my favourite pastime is listening in on the bus chat. This varies according to passenger type and bus route: the weather is a universally popular topic among pensioners, passing the hospital the mood changes to operations and gloom, and when the students get on the decibels rise and the humour returns. Sometimes the comments are racist, ageist or sexist – it all comes out with shocking disregard for other passengers in earshot.

Bus rides are seldom dull with their comings and goings and brief encounters between passengers, and this week's journeys have been particularly memorable.
My first bus journey of the week was on the Sunday morning before Christmas when I went into town alone, but unexpectedly started to experience "wearing off" symptoms. I gave up shopping and shuffled towards the nearest bus stop for the No. 26. I had taken my medication, but had to sit down and wait for it to kick in. I found myself sharing the bench with an alcoholic who immediately apologised for being inebriated. Punctuated with sips of vodka, he gave me a history of his addiction and the sad rejection by his close family. Just as he was about to discuss his marriage breakdown, the bus finally swung round the corner, much to my relief. Slowly, we stood up and walked unsteadily to get on it. I wanted to tell the bus driver that it was PD and not alcohol that made me unsteady, but he had probably heard it all before.

My second bus experience took place on the Thursday close to Christmas when I took the number 26 to the out-of-town DIY shop for a can of paint. I was feeling fine and within twenty minutes, my mission was accomplished and I headed back towards the bus stop to return home.

Once on the bus, I found a convenient aisle seat near the front so I could make an easy getaway. On approaching my bus stop, I stood up in good time to get my balance, but the bus lurched, my carrier bag-handle broke and almost two litres of matt emulsion spread over the floor and a couple of nearby passengers. For a moment I was lost for words, but then broke the bad news to the driver with gushing apologies. By this time, the bus was blocking the main road traffic and the driver had to call an emergency replacement bus. I did not wait to hear the outraged response from the rest of the passengers, but grabbed the half-empty can and headed hastily for home, my reactions accelerated by a burst of adrenaline. I had caused chaos with my "Spring Dawn" matt emulsion, but thank goodness I had not dropped a can of "Sunset Glow" in gloss, I reflected later when confessing to the bus company.

Calamities aside, I still rate public transport very highly and the bus has maintained my mobility. However, next time I am carrying paint or another risky substance I might splash out on a taxi instead.

9.6 Sleep problems with PD

Sleep problems are common among those with PD. If you experience poor sleep, it's important to talk to your doctor, as treating your sleep-related symptoms may improve your overall wellbeing.

The first step in dealing with your sleep problem is determining the root cause. If you have early or mid-stage PD, the chances are your sleep problems involve at least one of the following: insomnia, excessive daytime sleepiness, restless or shaky leg movements at night, intense dreams associated with rapid eye movement (REM) behaviour disorder (see below) or poor sleep due to depression.

While you will need professional medical assistance to determine what's causing your sleep problems, the following will help you understand what may be going on.

Insomnia
If you have insomnia, then you likely have a hard time getting a good night's sleep. Those with insomnia have trouble falling asleep, and may only sleep for a few hours at a time.

Somnolence (Excessive daytime sleepiness in PD)
Excessive daytime sleepiness is common in both early and mid-stage PD and may be related to insomnia. If you cannot get a good night's sleep, you are going to feel sleepy during the daytime. Sudden, irresistible daytime sleep attacks when you might fall asleep mid-conversation or, more seriously, when you are driving.

It is also possible to experience sudden and irresistible daytime "sleep attacks," which are a rare side effect of dopamine agonists pramipexole and ropinirole, as well as high doses of any dopaminergic drug (such as Sinemet, Madopar and Stalevo).

Restless legs syndrome (RLS)
Restless legs syndrome causes twitchy and unpleasant sensations in the legs. RLS causes sleep disturbance at night and frequently affects middle-aged and older people with PD.

REM sleep behaviour disorder (RBD)
Rapid eye movement (REM) sleep is the form of deep sleep where you have the most intense dreams. Usually, when you dream during REM sleep, nerve impulses going to your muscles are blocked so that you cannot act out your dreams. REM sleep behaviour disorder (RBD) can cause you to act out violent dreams, can also make it difficult to get a good night's sleep.

Depression in PD
Forty per cent of PWP experience depression during the course of the disease and will experience problems with sleep. In depression, sleep does not refresh you like it used to, or you wake up too early in the morning. Dreams for depressed people are different, too – they are rare and often depict a single image.

Sleep problems at later stages of PD
During the later stages of PD, you also may experience sleep problems related to higher doses of medications, such as hallucinations. As many as 33% of PD patients during mid- and later stages of the illness experience hallucinations, related to medication side effects. Hallucinations tend to occur visually (seeing things that are not really there) rather than audibly (hearing things that are not really there). They are frequently associated with vivid dreams.

Blog: Nodding off by Briony Cooke
This week has been a busy and tiring one with journeys, meetings and a conference. It is not surprising that I have been falling asleep at every opportunity: on the train, in the car and in public. One particularly tiring afternoon, I woke up just in time to avoid falling off my chair at a conference. I was not alone, and others were sleeping fitfully. I drifted off on several train journeys,

waking up with a start wondering if I had missed my station or whether the whole carriage had heard me snore. My Pilates class on Tuesday had some moments on concentrated activity when we stretched out our rigid muscles, but the moment we lay on our backs I dozed off, rudely missing the instructions.

Nodding off, snoozing or having forty winks (referred to medically as daytime somnolence or sudden sleep attacks) are habits I had planned to resist in middle age, until I got PD. If there was an Olympic medal for nodding off, I would get Gold. It has very little to do with boredom – I have even nodded off while in the middle of writing this paragraph but just for ten seconds. Like all of my PD symptoms, sudden sleep attacks are a nuisance and often embarrassing,

Somnolence is a well-recognised feature of PD and thought to be related to neurodegeneration and PD medication. Unlike the nodding off that hits many people after lunch, the attacks are sudden and can occur anytime and anywhere. For me, the most likely time is when my medication is working well. I have nodded off in many locations, but it usually happens when I am sitting comfortably in a warm room or a car with a dry atmosphere which causes my eyelids to drop.
I recollect first being affected by this not long after my diagnosis. It involved an irresistible urge to fall asleep, with very little warning. I would drift in and out of my dream world for a while and the distinction between being awake and being asleep became blurred. In my case, it was not real sleep, but a mental shutdown for just a few seconds during which time I could continue talking, eating or writing. I have fallen asleep mid-sentence while using voice recognition, and when I started 'sleep-marking' I realised it was time to give up teaching.
My husband is used to driving with a comatose passenger, but on several occasions, I have been awakened by the unexpected. Once

it was alarming to wake up in the middle of a ford that had turned into a raging torrent. It was quite surreal: a magical marital moment when I was lost for words as the car spluttered to a halt.

But nodding off in the car can have serious consequences for a driver as I discovered seven years after diagnosis. On this occasion, I woke up in a hedge having fallen asleep for just a few seconds, but enough to smash in the side of the car and knock down a large sign and push it 30 meters along the road. Fortunately, I had no injuries, neither did I experience any shock, presumably because I slept through the whole event. Some paramedics checked me over and the police breathalysed me, much to my youngest son's amusement when he arrived on the scene to help. I was none the worse for this accident.

The rest of that day, I felt fine, but that night I began to realise that falling asleep at the wheel was nothing new and many times I had yawned my way home through the rush-hour struggling to stay awake. This had been an accident waiting to happen, and next time I would not be so lucky. I discussed the risks of driving with my GP and we concluded that it was too risky for me to continue. I voluntarily surrendered my driving licence and have not missed driving thanks to my friends, family, and a fantastic local bus service.

9.7 Blog: Me and RBD (REM Sleep Behaviour Disorder) by Briony Cooke

Night-times have always been somewhat of a nightmare because sleep is elusive, but recent nightmares make daytime somnolence seem quite trivial. I have now begun to experience particularly vivid dreams and have to act them out. This sounds very amusing to watch, but the reality is quite disturbing.

Back in April 2017, I experienced the first of these events which have now become more frequent. The nightmare went like this: I was on the railway embankment near our local station and was scrambling desperately up the bramble-covered bank. My hands were torn and my legs were too weak to move. I looked to my left and I could see the front of the train hurtling towards me. It was terrifying and my shouting awoke my husband and he found me on the floor near the bedroom door. It took a while to get back to sleep (with the rattle of the early-morning trains going by), but eventually I managed it.

Since then I have been on several nocturnal field courses with my (ex) students. This time I am in a mountain range like the Andes. I am nervously tip-toeing along a narrow ridge with a precipitous drop on each side. The students have gone missing, I have no register and have broken scores of health and safety regulations. The footpath gives way and I am falling and falling. Then I wake up.

My falling out of bed is a regular happening and sometimes I have hit my head on the bedside cabinet. Our bedroom now looks like a gymnasium; a mattress on the floor to break my fall, 2 bed-handles that I might grab to steady myself on my way down and a rope attached to the bed leg to pull me up.

Other PD related problems such as acid reflux make it essential to be propped up on several pillows. This makes falling out of bed more likely. I can't win!

I have discussed this problem with my neurologist and he has recommended medication which will knock me out, but at least I shall feel rested in the morning. He warned me that I may not be able to do very much the morning after. I think I could tolerate any medication that will rescue me from oncoming trains and the shame of losing my register, students and dignity.

9 REVIEW
In dealing with each challenge – domesticating, retirement, travel and sleep - some solutions are offered by the contributors.
Key question
Suggest another type of challenge faced by PWP which involves practical difficulties. For example, dressing, eating, shopping, socialising.
Suggest coping strategies for each.

Chapter 10
Mustn't grumble

Introduction:
This chapter is about how we manage in spite of PD. There are several key strategies that determine how well we manage.
Distractions – these help us to put PD aside and reduce our anxiety levels.
Attitude – personality plays a part here and inevitably some PWP have a positive attitude while others are negative.

10.1 Distractions
Many people have hobbies which they are able to continue after a PD diagnosis, albeit in a modified way. Gardening may easily be continued for some years with the help of tools. Sports however may be too demanding especially of the first few years. Golf is one of the exceptions.
I have two main hobbies, both of which I continue years after diagnosis.
My distractions are: Keeping tortoises and singing.
My attitude is positive.

10.2 *Blog: Life in the slow lane by Briony Cooke*
Once upon a time I used to go to the local swimming pool at 8 o'clock on a Sunday morning and swim 40 lengths non-stop. Afterwards, Sundays were spent madly multi-tasking: cooking a roast dinner while supervising violin practice and cleaning out the hamster. My life was governed by principles, targets and deadlines. My favourite sayings were: "Time waits for no man (woman)", "She who hesitates is lost", and "The early bird gets the worm". I was always prepared and one step ahead of the game because I fantasised that was Superwoman – until my untimely diagnosis of PD killed that identity. For a while, I didn't know who I was.

It was shattering to be diagnosed with PD. I was in my forties with a job to hold down and children to support, but it should not have come as a surprise because I had already experienced typical symptoms for years. Slowness of movement and fumbling had become noticeable. My writing shrank in size, and it was an effort to write for any length of time without developing cramp (dystonia). Slowly and reluctantly, I came to accept that these impairments were a way of life, and I had to abandon the notion that anything was achievable. I was discovering the limits of my capabilities and learning to live with them long-term.

I continued to teach for six years post-diagnosis, but it was a struggle to keep the pace at times. In order to maintain standards or even improve my students' exam grades, I had to give up my weekends and abandon my leisure activities. Work began to encroach upon my sleep and I became exhausted. Retirement became inevitable and necessary.

After years of work and child-rearing, I have tried to look on the positive side and to regard retirement as an opportunity to revive old hobbies and develop new ones. I have taken up photography and am enjoying creative writing. I am also growing vegetables so that this year we will be self-sufficient.

PD has forced me to slow down, but this has given me time to think, listen, reflect, and appreciate those things that had once just passed me by. The priorities that drove me during my Superwoman years, such as progress, promotion and success, had been stress-inducing and no guarantee of happiness. The earliest benefit of retirement was a reduction of my medication and the chance to take more exercise and relax when I needed to. I was also very fortunate in having a supportive husband, family and friends around me.

My days are very different now and no longer driven by the clock; I can do things at my leisure. This afternoon I was sitting in the garden, closely observing my tortoise. She is huge, and I suspect she is pregnant, but her shell gets somewhat in the way. I am looking for other signs such as sniffing the ground and digging holes so that eventually I can detect where her nest is. Her afternoon was spent sunbathing, enjoying a strawberry or two, and then sleeping it off beneath the lavender bush. I admire her laid-back attitude to life and just watching her (in)activity is a form of therapy for me.

Tortoises make perfect pets for PWP because they move at our pace, hibernate when we are less active during the winter, need no walking, grooming or vaccinating, and are generally very accommodating. I have kept one or more tortoises since the age of three. I cannot imagine life without them. They have an endless archaic fascination.

Fig. 13 My distraction.
Source: Cooke archives.

The moral "Slow and steady wins the race" reflects my outlook on life these days. I am happy to be at the end of the Post Office queue, last off the bus, and to spend hours at the doctor's waiting room. PD has taught me to be a patient patient.

10.3 Emotions, endorphins and music
The ability that music has to affect and manipulate emotions and the brain is undeniable. The mechanism behind music's ability to physically influence the brain was not understood until relatively recently, and even now very little is known about the neurological effects of music.

Music can evoke several emotions. For example, major keys and rapid tempi cause happiness, whereas minor keys and slow tempi cause sadness, and rapid tempi together with dissonance cause fear. There is also a theory that dissonance sounds unpleasant to listeners across all cultures. Dissonance is to a certain degree culture-dependent, but also appears to be partly intrinsic to the music. Studies have shown that infants as young as four months old show negative reactions to dissonance.

A recent experiment dealt with this problem by attempting to minimise subjectivity, by measuring responses to dissonance. Music of varying dissonance was played for the subjects, while their cerebral blood flow was measured. Increased blood flow in a specific area of the brain corresponded with increased activity. It was found that the varying degrees of dissonance caused increased activity in the paralimbic regions of the brain, which are associated with emotional processes.

Another quantifiable aspect of emotional responses to music is its effect on hormone levels in the body There is evidence that music can lower levels of cortisol in the body (associated with arousal and stress), and raise levels of melatonin (which can induce sleep). This is outwardly visible in terms of music's ability to relax, to calm, and to give peace. Music is often used in the background hospitals to relax the patients. It also can cause the release of endorphins and can therefore help relieve pain.

Endorphins
The word "endorphin" consists of two parts - endo and orphin - which are short forms of the words endogenous and morphine, intended to mean "a morphine-like substance originating from within the body." The term "endorphin rush" has been adopted in popular speech to refer to feelings of exhilaration brought on by pain, danger, or other forms of stress, supposedly due to the influence of endorphins. When a nerve impulse reaches the spinal cord, endorphins are released which prevent nerve cells from releasing more pain signals.

Endorphins can:
Relieve pain
Enhance the immune system
Reduce stress levels
Postpone the ageing process
Modulate appetite
Lower blood pressure
Induce a calm or euphoric state of mind

10.4 *Blog: Music, Music, Music by Briony Cooke*
Music has always been important to me: I started recorder lessons at the age of eight with mother Mary Magdalene, a nun at my convent school. I then moved on to the violin and scraped my way through several exams and made it to the back row of the second fiddles in the local youth orchestra. However, my real passion was always singing. I enjoyed singing in the school choir, but the lack of boys was a distinct disadvantage, and at the age of

15 *I had to suffer the indignity of being the leading boy in Gilbert and Sullivan's Trial by Jury.*

Singing has been an unconscious and compulsive habit of mine which my family have tolerated but others have found irritating. This truth came home to me as a student while working in a hospital kitchen with a group of three work-weary women. As a penance for being young and a bit too happy, they gave me the unenviable task of scrubbing soup and porridge pans. Then one day, while I was scouring and singing away, one of the staff came by asking "Is it difficult to sing like that?" I was flattered until she added "Because it ain't half difficult to listen to!" I continued scrubbing and turned the volume up in defiance. This comment was not going to knock me off my perch.
When I started university, I joined the King's College Choir in London where there were altos, tenors and basses which made singing much more interesting. Between the ages of 20 and 40, singing was my main leisure pursuit: I sang Handel's Messiah in St Paul's Cathedral, and met my husband in a choir at Westminster Cathedral. The high point for me was when I performed Verdi's Requiem with him in the Albert Hall. All this was in my pre-PD days.

The diagnosis of PD swept away my self-confidence and the last thing I wanted to do was to stand on stage and perform in a concert. I felt that I was unable to control my PD symptoms which were driven mainly by unfounded anxiety. I imagined drawing attention to myself by fumbling with my score and dropping it, or worse still fainting due to low blood pressure which I had done before. It was not worth making a fool of myself and I decided to stay out of the limelight and gave up the choir in 2000. It was the leisure activity I most enjoyed and I was left with humming around the house. The frustration was most intense when sitting in the audience listening to a performance which I could have been part of: knowing the songs, note for note, and humming them quietly to myself.

Early in 2012, I heard of a choir which would be ideal for me and a friend who also had PD who was keen to start singing again. The conductor was most welcoming and appreciative of PD symptoms, and the two of us became members. He was a pianist and a singer with an excellent baritone voice who would demonstrate how to use our voices effectively. There are many aspects of singing which are therapeutic. It began to help me with verbal articulation, intonation and volume which all require diaphragm and breath control. I now began to develop more power in my voice, my breathing was less shallow, and as a soprano I could reach those top notes once again. Following the score and sight reading are skills that I revived, and this mental discipline was another benefit of singing.

Rehearsals started at 19:30 and ended two hours later – this required stamina and a fair amount of forward planning. To avoid going 'off' during the evening, I took my medication on an empty stomach half an hour before the rehearsal, had a drink in the break and had my evening meal when I got home. Although rehearsals were long and demanding, I felt full of enthusiasm at the end of the evening and the reward far outweighed the effort. Singing is like a tonic – it results in the release of endorphins and, like eating curry or taking exercise, it made me feel good.

Since moving out of a large town, I have joined the local church choir which has been very enjoyable. The practices on Friday evenings are not too long and the services manageable. PD imposes a couple of difficulties; breathing and standing. It's mainly a matter of keeping my mind on the job and planning my medication carefully; running out of dopamine midway could be disastrous. The choir members have been very supportive especially during my recovery from two brain operations and I have learnt a great deal about music. This has been my therapy for the last four years.

Fig. 14 St. Thomas's Choir after Evensong at Christ Church Cathedral, Oxford. August 2017.
Source: Robin Middleton.

10.5 PD and Personality
Some common personality traits such as ambition and rigidity have been noted in people with PD. Many experts on Parkinson's, including spouses of those with the condition, believe that people with the condition develop certain distinctive personality traits and that these traits appear long before the onset of the physical symptoms of Parkinson's.

Observers of people with PD — even observers who lived more than 100 years ago — have reported that those suffering from PD tend to be:
Ambitious
Industrious
Serious
Single-minded
Rigid

Introverted
Slow-tempered

These personality traits seem to appear years before physical PD symptoms appear, and there may be a reason for it: the loss of dopamine, a chemical made by your brain cells that helps both to regulate your physical movements and your emotional responses.

PD and dopamine
The brains of people with PD don't make enough dopamine. When levels of dopamine drop low enough, the physical symptoms of the condition appear. But it's also possible that this loss of dopamine starts years before those symptoms begin, but that it has subtle effects on the personality.

Since dopamine is the brain chemical that allows you to feel energy, pleasure, and thrills, it follows that if you are low on dopamine, you may become more introverted and less willing to take risks for a thrill.

Parkinson's personality traits and medications
People with PD tend not to smoke or to engage in other risky health behaviours until they are medicated with dopamine agonists, which are PD drugs that mimic the effects of dopamine in the brain.

In some people, these drugs actually lead to another personality change: the person taking them starts to take too many risks, perhaps by gambling or engaging in unusual sexual behaviour.

This personality turnaround may be dramatic and even could threaten the wellbeing of the person with Parkinson's and his or her family.

Therefore, it's important to be aware of potential personality changes when starting a new PD drug.

Parkinson's and Adolf Hitler
There's speculation that Adolf Hitler may have suffered from Parkinson's disease — by the end of his life in 1945, he had a major tremor in his left hand. At least one study suggests that Hitler's disease and his so-called "Parkinson's personality" may have contributed to Germany's defeat in World War II.
In that study, a team of neurologists speculated that Hitler's "questionable and risky decision-making and his inhumane and callous personality" both were influenced and magnified by Parkinson's disease. Food for thought.

10.6 Attitudes:
Optimism
We are often told by members of the "well" world to stay positive. You may be asking why you have this responsibility of keeping the world laughing when you are suffering. It is particularly annoying when you have just been diagnosed and well-meaning friends tell you to "think positive". At that stage, you have nothing to feel positive about and you are wondering what gives them the right to dictate to you how you should feel. Winston Churchill had a famous quote that "a pessimist sees the difficulty in every opportunity; an optimist sees the opportunity in every difficulty." This section defines optimism, examines its origin and type and its influence upon the gravity and progression of a chronic illness such as PD.

Research has shown that optimism is correlated with many positive life outcomes. These include:
Increased life expectancy
Better physical health
Better mental health
Improved immune system
Prevention of chronic disease
Increased success in sports and work
Greater recovery rates from heart operations
Better coping strategies when faced with adversity.

Although healthier lifestyles play a big part in avoiding some of the deadlier diseases, researchers think the single most important factor is a positive mental attitude.

Defining optimism
Dispositional optimism has been defined as a global expectation that more good (desirable) things than bad (undesirable) will happen in the future (by Scheier and Carver, 1985). As a personality trait, it is presumed to be stable with little scope for change.

Unrealistic optimism (Weinstein, 1989) describes the objective mismatch between the expectations of dispositional optimism and actual evidence about the probability of such life events occurring.
Optimistic people are happier, receive more social support, are less stressed and are less depressed. Of all the areas studied in the relatively young field of positive psychology, gratitude has perhaps the widest body of research. Grateful people have been shown to have greater levels of positive effect, a greater sense of belonging, and lower levels of depression and stress.

Generating gloom – the losses

People who have recently been diagnosed PD anticipate a number of losses which in themselves can lead to depression and pessimism. Many illnesses involve loss and PD is no exception. Losses can be experienced through the course of the disease and the number of perceived losses will vary between individuals.

Physical losses	**Emotional losses**	**Tangible losses**
Balance	Confidence	Employment
Stamina	Purpose	Earnings
Control	Drive	Friendships
Dexterity	Humour	
Articulation	Skills	
Facial expression		

The two divergent routes and their associated attitudes are shown below. Optimism is the ideal, but it is not in the nature of some people to be optimistic and they find this very hard if they are the victims of PD as well.

Route of the optimist	**Route of the Pessimist**
Keep working as long as I can.	Give up work straight away.
Get out and socialise.	Stay at home
Maintain old friendships.	Give up friendships
Look after myself physically.	Self-neglect
Develop new hobbies.	Give up old hobbies
Join a support group.	Avoid others especially PWP.
Optimise sleep.	Dread the night-times

Self-help - Ways of adopting a more optimistic outlook

What do you do if you are not naturally optimistic? The good news is that optimism can be learned. Leading researcher Eric

Kim* says there are several exercises we can introduce into our daily lives to help engender positive thinking. One is to keep in mind "your best possible self", the one who has achieved all your personal and professional goals; another is to write down three things for which you are grateful every day; and the third is to keep a log of all the little acts of kindness you do for others. Practising mindfulness meditation can also help, he says.
Looking at the mind again, in the USA antidepressants are not working for more than half the people suffering from severe and chronic depression. Adopting a more optimistic attitude may substitute for medication.
Chocolate is one of my favourite indulgences and a source of pleasure, therefore I feel it should appear in this chapter. It fulfils both of my aims at the start of this chapter, to cheer up and think about something else – chocolate.
*https://www.academia.edu/13922732/Changes_in_optimism_are_associated_with_changes_in_health_over_time_among_older_adults
http://www.academia.edu/27207799/Health_happiness_and_mortality

10.7 Blog: *The emotional value of chocolate*, by Briony Cooke
For many of us, January is a grim month of reflection rather than hope, and we resolve to give up those things we enjoy but do us no good. My resolution is always to give up chocolate, and every year I fail. I could write at length about all its virtues: its exquisite taste, smooth texture, those melting moments, and the need to have another piece – one is never enough. Willpower is not my strong point, and the lifetime of a bar of chocolate in my care is very short. I am not proud of my chocolate addiction, and need to get this under control if only to spare my waistline and my teeth.

Outside the home temptation abounds, and my favourite brands are all too readily available in the village where I live – it's no trouble at all slipping a small bar into my bag (remembering to pay for it first). The station platform is also a favourite venue for chocolate consumption. To wait for the train in front of a chocolate vending machine without succumbing would be impossible. I can justify a quick snack any time: I need to keep up my blood sugar for the forthcoming journey and never mind the extra calories because I will burn them off on two sets of stairs on the journey. Calories out to balance calories in, I think to myself as I put my one pound into the machine and grovel in the bottom to retrieve my favourite bar.

I am not one to lie back on a comfy armchair guzzling chocolate while watching TV. I prefer to eat chocolate on the go. That's not to say I would never indulge while on the sofa, but at the same time I might stroke the cat or do the crossword which also uses calories in thought processes, I reason to myself. On the whole, I prefer my own company when eating chocolate because I feel guilty and greedy, and of course I might have to share!

Although this behaviour is selfish, shameful and immature, I can find some justification for it. I have read that PWPs tend to eat more chocolate than the population as a whole because many claim that it improves their walking and makes them feel good. I could argue that having an incurable chronic disease gives me the licence to over-indulge in one of life's pleasures as a form of compensation. This is a pretty good excuse, but it still doesn't solve the problem of the expanding waistline.

Just as I was turning over these questions in my mind recently, I discovered some exciting *new research that identifies several good reasons for eating chocolate: it improves blood flow to the brain and therefore thinking skills; it is good for the heart; and controls blood sugar levels. For PWP there are some specific benefits: it improves mobility and enhances the mood. So, eating

chocolate is good for you – but in moderation, and that is the hard bit. For me it's all or nothing; I could cope better with cutting out chocolate entirely rather than cutting down because the latter does nothing to cure the addiction and even just an occasional mouthful would revive the craving.
My resolve to give up chocolate was knocked completely by the results of a routine medical last month which revealed that my weight (Body Mass Index) was within the normal range, my cholesterol was low and my blood pressure that of a 20-year-old. I was described as very fit and low risk. It appears that my lifestyle is near perfect and therefore to exclude chocolate would be a big mistake.

I am on a treacherous chocolate-covered slippery slope with this dilemma. On the one hand chocolate makes me feel good, on the other it makes me fat. I'll have another piece while I try to resolve this!
Yes, with the nuts, please.

*http://www.telegraph.co.uk/health-fitness/nutrition/chocolate-10-health-reasons-you-should-eat-more-of-it/

10.8
Blog: Looking on the bright side, by Briony Cooke
When I was first diagnosed with PD in 2000 I had a chat with the leader of the local support group who said that whatever I did I must stay optimistic as a way of accepting my condition. Instead of asking myself "Why me?", I should ask myself "Why not me?" At the time, I was still stunned by the diagnosis and not very receptive to this advice. I didn't feel the least bit optimistic and I thought it grossly unfair that I'd been dealt this card. I wrote in my diary that this nasty disease was going to "cramp my style, crush my spirit and isolate me". At the time, there was very little support in our neighbourhood and no access to a PD Nurse, so I was very much on my own. It was hard work keeping my job as a

teacher and trying to maintain the morale of my students when mine was so undermined.

However, once I was on a stable medication regime my confidence began to return and I started to accept that PD was not going to rule my life. I knew that I could not stop the progression, but I would attempt to cope with the infinite challenges it brought. But the most profound improvement was in self-esteem and I stopped seeing myself as a victim. I set up a young onset support group, became less self-centred and I adopted a positive attitude. Instead of casting other people down with negative thoughts about the future, I would demonstrate to the newly-diagnosed how life with PD had not cramped my style and we still had opportunities.

Optimism is an attitude that doesn't develop naturally, but must be cultivated. First, you have to recognise those activities that improve your mood. For me, keeping active makes me feel normal, and every day I make sure I get out and have some exercise. This may be informal exercise such as walking into town or doing some gardening or perhaps more formalised through Pilates and hydrotherapy classes. But, without exception, participation in exercise raises my spirits and makes me feel physically better.

During the last two years I have belonged to a singing group. This is an informal gathering in the sitting room of a friend of mine, where about 15 of us sing a variety of music from classical to pop accompanied by a very talented pianist and baritone. Even though he works us hard for two hours, which involves a lot of strenuous singing and standing, I am still going strong by 9.30 pm when normally I'm burning out and going off. On Monday evenings, I could party all night! It seems that a pleasurable activity such as singing releases endorphins, which are mood-

enhancing. The more singing I do the better I feel. From what I have read, controlled breathing, articulation and social enjoyment are all reasons why singing is so beneficial and its effect long-lasting.

Optimism also stems from having things to look forward to. In 2014, I was looking forward to becoming a grandparent, which was a thrilling prospect. There is nothing like a new baby for making us reflect on the great things in life. Until recently, my one fear was that I would never see my grandchildren or I may not be able to play with them because of my physical limitations, but this no longer applies. I am not yet a shaking wreck, I can still walk even though very badly at times and I'm quite able to look after grandchildren up to a point.

"Why not me?" is a question that I now appreciate, and I realise that some close friends who are ill have to bear far greater suffering than me and their prognosis is much worse. Picking out the positives, PD usually progresses very slowly which gives us time to cope with new symptoms. It could all be so much worse and I have learnt to live with the uncertain future and to enjoy the present.

10.9
A Tribute to Tom Isaacs

Tom Isaacs was founder of the Cure Parkinson's Trust and I first talked to him in 2007 when we discussed ways of promoting the views of the PWP. Putting the patient first was fundamental to his approach to dealing with this illness and it was very heartening to know that he was listening to us and of course, he was one of us. I had the greatest admiration for Tom. He was diagnosed at 26 and sadly he died in 2017 aged 49. His energy was phenomenal, but above all I shall remember him for his enthusiasm for life and his conviction that a cure for PD would be found. He always looked on the bright side.

Fig. 15 Source: Lyndsey Isaacs.

Lyndsey and Tom Isaacs at the Mike Tindall Golf Day at The Belfry on 19th May 2017 - 12 days before he died, he was doing something he loved.

CHAPTER 10 REVIEW
This chapter considers attitude as an influential factor upon how well you live with PD. Some people are born with a cheerful disposition, while others find adversity more difficult to cope with and have to learn how to acquire it; this is hard. Tom Isaacs was wonderfully optimistic and an example to all of us.

Chapter 11
Parkinson's: a laughing matter

11.1 Parky Games

PD is no joke, but we have no choice and it is a route we have to follow so we might as well follow it cheerfully. Laughter is certainly a tonic and makes you feel good. If you prefer to move on now that's fine. There may come a time when you want to poke fun at this disease and get your own back.
This section is devoted to funny side of having PD.
There are games and competitions which might liven up a PD Support meeting or a party.
It also gives you things to do think about while you are "off" and unable to do anything else.

The anagram
RISK NO NAPS
There are some other very good and easy anagrams you get from the word - PARKINSONS. Search for Anagrams on the internet.

Poetry
Still in the word business. Many of the words associated with PD symptoms have a similar sound. Perhaps a short poem might come to mind?
You may have noticed that there are many words associated with PD which rhyme with **Fumble** (and we do plenty of that!) In your team, you could write a poem.

No wrinkles
PD has a physical impact and when under- medicated we look sad. A look in the bathroom mirror at 2 am will confirm this, but don't worry because medication will put it right tomorrow. One compensation for the deadpan face is that lack of smiling reduces

the amount of lines in your face, politely called "laughter lines" This means fewer wrinkles. PD is such a blessing! I imagine you might be saying now "I'd rather have the wrinkles, but not the PD".

Competitions
You could also introduce a quiz using the glossary in this book. You could play Parky Scrabble with bonuses or any word that is associated with this condition.

11.2
Achievements

Fig. 16
Sebastian and Edith Cooke – grandchildren.
    Source – Linden and Antony Cooke

My ambition has been to have grandchildren and to play with them. At one stage this seemed improbable. Having DBS has improved my physical capabilities and quality of life and the dream of playing with grandchildren has been fulfilled.

When I look back on the last two decades, they have been good. PD has offered me opportunities, not obstacles.

Opportunities
Through having PD, I have met some inspirational people with drive and energy despite PD. Our paths would not have crossed otherwise.

Having PD has improved my resilience: tomorrow is another day. I like to keep this in mind when things are getting rough.

Early retirement from teaching has allowed me to become an author.

Writing about PD in general has made me realise that I am relatively lucky.

PD has given me the chance to speak on national and local radio.

So, would I be happier now without PD?
NO!

Final conclusions
Here are the principal points in Chapters 2-11 that will give you a formula for surviving Parkinson's

2 Diagnosis raises many questions about your future. Do not be afraid to seek answers.

3 Brace yourself for the range of responses to your diagnosis and react sympathetically.

4 Knowledge is powerful and allows you to engage in debate and to raise public awareness of PD.

5 Taking control means following medical advice and maintaining your general health irrespective of PD.

6 Be courageous and open your mind to the choices offered to you.

7 Acknowledge that PD is a progressive disease and make the most of now. Investigate those opportunities offered to you.

8 Be aware that your mood influences your physical well-being. Optimism is essential.

9 Acknowledge your limitations and be prepared for adventures.

10 The key to survival:
Keep busy
Look on the bright side of life.

11 Keep smiling.

GLOSSARY

Amantadine: A medication used to treat PD as a single therapy or with L-DOPA and other medications. It has both an anti-PD effect and an anti-dyskinesia effect.

Ataxia: Inability to coordinate voluntary muscle movements; unsteady movements and staggering gait.

Autonomic Nervous System (ANS): Part of the peripheral nervous system, consisting of sympathetic and parasympathetic nerves that control involuntary actions, in particular the heart, smooth muscle (such as bladder and blood vessels) and glands.

Basal ganglia: A region deep within the brain consisting of large bundles of neurons responsible for voluntary movement.

Blood-brain barrier: The separating membrane between the blood and the brain; a tight physical barrier that normally keeps immune cells, chemicals and drugs out of the brain.

Bradykinesia: Literally, means slowness of movement. It is commonly used synonymously with akinesia and hypokinesia. Bradykinesia is a clinical hallmark of Parkinsonism.

Carbidopa: A drug given with Levodopa. Carbidopa blocks the enzyme dopa decarboxylase, thereby preventing Levodopa from being metabolized to dopamine. Because Carbidopa does not penetrate the blood-brain barrier (see above), it only blocks Levodopa metabolism in the peripheral tissues and not in the brain, thereby reducing side effects but increasing the effectiveness of Levodopa.

Central nervous system (CNS). This refers to the region of the spinal chord and brain.

Chronic: (opposite: acute) chronic diseases are of long duration. They are typically of subtle onset and slow worsening over time. The term does not imply anything about the severity of a disease.

Cognitive dysfunction: The loss of intellectual functions such as thinking, reasoning, making judgments and remembering.

Complementary therapies: These are non-medical treatments, which many people use in addition to conventional medical treatments. They include aromatherapy, music and art therapies, reflexology and osteopathy.

CT or CAT scan (Computerised tomography). This uses a series of x-rays to create an image. A two-dimensional image is created by obtaining "slices" of the body from different directions.

Deep Brain Stimulation (DBS): A surgical treatment that involves the implantation of a neurostimulator (a pulse generator) which sends electrical pulses to parts of the brain, for example, the STN (subthalamic nucleus). The pulses are delivered by 2 electrodes. These correct the faulty mechanisms of neurotransmission in PD.

Dementia: A decline in memory and /or intellectual function. This may affect some PWP with more advanced disease. The symptoms do not respond to PD medication.

Dopamine: A small chemical molecule that is one of the brain's neurotransmitters. It is found particularly in cells within the substantia nigra. These cells project to the striatum in the basal ganglia. Deficiency of dopamine causes symptoms of PD.

Dopamine agonist: A compound that activates dopamine receptors, other than dopamine. Examples include, bromocriptine mesylate (Parlodel), pergolide (Permax), pramipexole (Mirapexin), ropinirole hydrochloride (Requip), piribedil, cabergoline, apomorphine (Apokyn), rotigotine (Neupro patch) and Lisuride. These act like dopamine, but are not actually dopamine. They can be used in both the early and late stages of PD. They are the second most powerful type of anti-Parkinson medication after Levodopa. They can cause side effects such as sleepiness, insomnia, ankle swelling, hallucinations and obsessive compulsive disorders (OCDs).

Dysarthria: Impaired speech function.

Dyskinesia: Abnormal involuntary movements. These are a side-effect of long-term Levodopa use.

Dysphagia: Difficulty in swallowing. This has the effect of drooling when saliva accumulates in the mouth. It can also lead to the inhalation of food or liquids which in advanced cases can lead to aspiration pneumonia and death.

Dystonia: A movement disorder that may be associated with PD. Dystonia is characterised by abnormal or awkward posture or sustained movement of hands, feet and other parts of the body. It may be accompanied by rigidity and twisting.

Entacapone: A PD drug that is used alongside Levodopa and Carbidopa. It inhibits the enzyme COMT, decreasing the breakdown of Levodopa.

GP: General medical practitioner – normally the first patient contact for PWP in the UK.

Idiopathic PD: This term is used to describe the common type of PD to distinguish it from other forms of Parkinsonism.

Levodopa (L-DOPA): A chemical that is the precursor to dopamine. It can pass through the blood-brain barrier (whereas dopamine cannot). Once it has entered the central nervous system, L-dopa is converted into dopamine by aromatic L-amino acid decarboxylase (DOPA decarboxylase/DDC). L-DOPA is also converted into dopamine within the peripheral nervous system.

Magnetic resonance imaging (MRI): A non-invasive medical imaging technique to visualize detailed internal structure and limited function of the body. MRI provides much greater contrast between the different soft tissues of the body than computerised tomography (CT), making it especially useful in neurological (brain), musculoskeletal, cardiovascular and oncological (cancer-related) imaging.

Motor symptoms: Symptoms that involve movement, coordination, physical tasks or mobility. These include, among others: resting tremor, bradykinesia, rigidity, postural instability, freezing, micrographia, mask-like expression, unwanted accelerations, stooped posture, dystonia, impaired motor dexterity, coordination, speech problems, difficulty swallowing, muscle cramping, and drooling of saliva. (Also see Non-motor symptoms)

Neurological conditions: Disorders caused by damage of malfunctioning of the brain or central nervous system.

Neurologist: A doctor who specializes in the diagnosis, care and treatment of disorders of the brain or nervous system.

Neurotransmitter: A chemical messenger in the nervous system that permits communication between two neuronal cells, normally across a synapse. The neurotransmitter is released from the nerve terminals on the axons. Examples of neurotransmitters include dopamine, acetylcholine.

Non-motor symptoms: Symptoms that do not involve movement, coordination, physical tasks or mobility, including loss of sense of smell, constipation, sleep disorders or disturbances, mood disorders, orthostatic hypotension, bladder problems, sexual problems, excessive saliva, weight loss or gain, vision and dental problems, fatigue, depression, fear and anxiety, skin problems and cognitive issues. (See also Motor symptoms)

On and Off: The clinical states of PD while being treated with Levodopa, which commonly cause fluctuations after a few years of treatment. The "on" state is when the PD symptoms and signs are reduced by Levodopa. The "off" state is when the benefit has been reduced or lost. The most common type of "off" is wearing-off, due to the Levodopa's benefit not lasting more than 3- 4 hours after a dose.

PD: Parkinson's Disease.

PWP: Person(s) with PD.

Restless leg syndrome (RLS): A neurological disorder characterised by unpleasant sensations in the legs, like the feeling of ants crawling underneath the skin. These sensations usually occur in the late evening and during sleep. Walking around relieves the sensation, hence the term "restless legs."

Rigidity: A special type of muscle stiffness, which is one of the main symptoms of PD. The muscles tend to pull against each other instead of working smoothly together.

Subthalamic nucleus (STN): A small lens-shaped nucleus involved in movement control. It is part of the basal ganglia. It receives input from the cerebral cortex and from the globus pallidus interna. It is "overactive" in PD due to loss of inhibitory incoming fibres. It is a common target in deep brain stimulation for PD.

Unified Parkinson's Disease Rating Scale (UPDRS): A rating scale used to measure the severity of PD. The UPDRS can follow a person's worsening condition over time and also measure improvement with various treatments.
This updated scale has modified the origin.
The MDS-UPDRS has four parts, namely:
Non-motor experiences of daily living.
Motor experiences of daily living.
Motor examination
Motor complications
Twenty questions on each are completed by the patient / caregiver.

APPENDIX
Financial benefits for PWP (UK only).
To find out your eligibility for benefits you should contact the DWP (Department of Work and Pensions), Helpful organisations which can assist you in the application process include Disability Rights (Online) Benefits and Work (Online). If you do not have access to a computer, Citizens Advice Bureau is very helpful.
Attendance Allowance is available if you're aged 65 or over and you need help with personal care or someone to watch over you to

make sure you're safe. It's based on the help you need, not on the help you actually get – you don't need to have someone looking after you to qualify.

Personal Independence Payment (PIP) is a relatively new benefit for people between the ages of 16 and 64 with a long-term illness or disability. PIP has two parts: a daily-living component if you need help with everyday activities and a mobility component if you have difficulty getting around.

Disability Living Allowance provides help towards the extra costs of bringing up a disabled child. Before PIP was introduced from 2013, disabled adults under 65 could also claim. If you still receive this benefit as an adult, you will be reassessed at some point for transfer to PIP.

Carer's Allowance is for people who regularly spend 35 hours a week or more caring for someone with substantial caring needs. You do not have to be related to or live with the person you care for. You'll also get National Insurance credits to help towards your State Pension.

Carer's Credit is intended to protect the State Pension and bereavement benefit rights of carers who are not able to pay National Insurance contributions and are not entitled to Carer's Allowance.

N.B. Those who turned 65 after April 2013 and have been in receipt of DLA will be contacted and asked if they would like to apply for PIP

Specialists and how to contact them (UK)

Title	Role	Accessing Service
Physiotherapist	Exercises to reduce rigidity, improve walking and balance.	Referral by GP
Speech therapist	Improves tone and volume> Reduces swallowing problems.	Referral by GP
Occupational therapist	Assesses the risks in your home and arranges installation of equipment which increase safety.	Referral by GP or neurologist.
Social worker	Provides information on benefits and will review family problems.	
Psychotherapist / counsellor	A listener when you cannot sort out a problem without help.	Referral by GP.
Parkinson's Nurse Practitioner	Provides information on PD, medication and DBS follow-up (If available)	Referral by GP or neurologist.
Dietician	Advice on diet to avoid constipation, weight gain and weight loss. Also, the consumption of protein to avoid absorption problems with Levodopa.	Referral by GP.

Some useful contacts

Parkinson's Australia
www.parkinsons.org.au
Infoline: 1800 644 189

Associação Brasil Parkinson
Av. Bosque de Saúde 1155
Saúde
São Paulo
SP 04142-092
Brazil
Tel: (11) 2578 8177
www.parkinson.org.br

Hong Kong Parkinson's Disease Association
Ground Floor,
Wang Lai House,
Wang Tau Hom Estate,
Kowloon
Tel: 2337 2292
Email: hkpda@netvigator.com
www.hkpda.org

Parkinson's Disease and Movement Disorder Society (India)
Room 131,
MRC Bombay Hospital,
12 Marine Lines,
Mumbai 400020
Tel +91 22 66 106 249
Email pdms.india@gmail.com

AMPAC – Asociacion Mexicana de Parkinson
Av. Emiliano Zapata 115,
Col. Portales (Metro Ermita)
Tel: 52 43 94 36
Email: ampac.parkinson@gmail.com
www.ampacmexico.com

Parkinson's Association South Africa
Jackal Creek Golf Estate,
2194 Honeydew
Gauteng
Tel: +27 84 650 6500
www.parkinsonssa.org

Parkinson's UK
216 Vauxhall Bridge Rd,
London, SWIV 1EJ
   Tel: 020 7931 8080
http://www.parknsons.org.uk
National helpline 0808 800 0303

European Parkinson's Disease Association (EPDA)
1, Cobden Rd,
Sevenoaks, Kent TN13 3UB,
UK
http://www.epda.eu.com/en/PD

American Parkinson's Disease Association
135 Parkinson Avenue,
Staten Island,
New York,
NY 10305
http://apdaparkinson.org

National Parkinson Foundation (USA)
200 SE 1st Street, Suite 800,
Miami,
Florida,33131.
http://www.parkinson.org

Michael J Fox Foundation for Parkinson's Research (USA).
Grand Central Station, PO Box 4777,
New York,
NY 10163-4777
http://www.michaeljfox.org

Cure Parkinson's Trust
120, Baker Street,
Marylebone,
London W1U 6TU
UK
http://www.cureparkinsonstrust.org.uk

Printed in Great Britain
by Amazon